Jacob K. Huff

Songs of the Desert

Jacob K. Huff

Songs of the Desert

ISBN/EAN: 9783743315211

Manufactured in Europe, USA, Canada, Australia, Japa

Cover: Foto ©Thomas Meinert / pixelio.de

Manufactured and distributed by brebook publishing software
(www.brebook.com)

Jacob K. Huff

Songs of the Desert

SONGS
OF THE
DESERT

BY
FARAWAY MOSES
(JACOB HUFF.)

AUTHOR'S APOLOGY.

———

SINCE it is the custom of authors to write a sort of apologetic preface for their works, I will work one into mine, although I do not know what I could say that would make the stuffing of the book suit the taste of those who have no taste for verse.

Almost everybody will be disappointed in this book, because they have been expecting something humorous. But there is a sad and serious side to every man's life, and in mine there has been a homesick feeling haunting my soul since I came West, and, while roaming over the deserts of Colorado, where the silence feels as heavy and gloomy as the shadow of death, these songs came into my heart like requiems sung over the graves where I am fast burying the memories of my boyhood friends; for the many faces I loved in the long ago seem to be fading away from Memory's view, like the little whirlwinds of sand that go dancing out towards the horizon and disappear forever.

My next book will be in prose, giving the humorous, pathetic and wicked sides of Western life, and will be my master-work. I have been already two years collecting material for this book, and it will take one year more to complete the work. It will be called

"THE MORTAL CINCH;
A TALE OF THE
SINS AND SORROWS OF THE WILD AND WICKED WEST."

Look out for it in the near future.

FARAWAY MOSES.
(JACOB HUFF.)

INDEX.

SONGS OF THE DESERT.

OUT ON THE DESERT.

Were you ever on the desert,
　　out on Colorado's plains?
Where the sun shines hot all Summer,
　　and it very seldom rains ;
Where the grease wood and the salt-sage
　　are the only living thing,
Except some lonely flowers
　　in the early months of Spring ;
And the prairie-dog and rabbit,
　　and the raven's lonely "caw,"
And the air so sad with silence
　　that it fills your soul with awe.
Oh, it's awful tramping over
　　through the silence strange and odd,
And the sun-rays pouring on you
　　like the vengeance of your God.
There are mountains all around you,
　　in the distance looking blue,
With their peaks in the horizon,
　　just as tho' they'd stabbed it through ;

And the highest covered over
    with a coat of ice and snow,
So far above the timber-line
    where trees can never grow ;
And they look so strange and dreary
    looming up so high and odd—
Look as tho' they frowned upon you,
    and were lonelier than God :
And you wonder if they stood there
    through so many million years,
And were always cold and lonely
    and unmoved by human tears.
And the winds rush by so silent,
    sending dust clouds in the air,
For there's no trees, with their branches,
    to obstruct the passage there ;
And the sky seems far and distant,
    painted in the deepest blue,
And there's not the smallest cloudlet
    to obstruct the distant view.
But the silence, oh, the silence !
    fills your soul with nameless fears,
And your heart is aching, aching,
    filled with dreams of former years ;
And the dry plains, parch'd and barren,
    and the sand-hills standing bare,
Here and there the bones of cattle
    bleaching in the silent air:
And you wonder if in Heaven
    God remembers this lone place.
If he looks on it in pity,

seeing it in the embrace
Of this awful, death-like silence,
    and the great sun's burning rays;
Where all nature cries for water
    through the burning summer days :
And you wonder if the angels
    know how all these cattle died
Of thirst and grim starvation,
    on this desert parch'd and dried ;
And your heart grows sad and heavy
    as you onward silent plod,
Looking to the far-off mountains,
    standing lonely as their God.
But yet, with all its horrors,
    and its dreadful, barren state,
Men are trying to reclaim it,
    even tho' the task is great ;
For there seems to be a hunger
    in the human heart for land,
And the poor men, who are driven
    from their homes with empty hand,
Will now face this dreadful silence,
    and, where nature does oppose,
Will, by careful irrigation,
    bloom this desert like the rose :
And the mountains over yonder
    watching these poor people plod,
Will know they feel the silence,
    and are lonelier than God.

CHARLIE.

In the Spring time when we parted,
I remember how love smarted,
And she left me broken-hearted,
  For her parents frowned on me.
To the far West they did take her,
Thinking I would then forsake her,
But this promise I did make her:
  Charlie, I will come for thee!

Oh, the sad and weary waiting,
And my poor heart nearly breaking;
No one else could feel the aching,
  Nor the shadows could they see.
But the years went slowly crawling,
Thrice the Winter snows came falling,
And my heart was ever calling:
  Charlie, I will come for thee!

In the twilight shadows falling,
And the Coyote's dismal calling,
And the weary cattle bawling,
  Pictures Western life to me.
On the old Ute reservati n,
There is one sage-brush plantation;
From the little railroad station
  Charlie's new home one can see.

To this cabin I'm advancing,
While my blood goes through me dancing,
Visions my poor heart entrancing,
  For my loved one I can see.
To the gate with one hand clinging—
Hark, I hear her sweet voice singing :
To the new moon she is singing
  "Bring my loved one back to me!"

"Both my parents have relented,
And their cruel deed repented,
And to-day they both consented
  My loved one dare come to me.
All our fortune has departed,
And the old folks broken-hearted—"
At these words I cried and started :
  "Charlie, I have come for thee!"

———

No more words were spoke at meeting,
For our true hearts, wildly beating,
Smothered ev'ry tender greeting,
  While I held her close to me.
And the stars in Heaven shining,
Smiled to see our arms entwining ;
There shall be no more repining—
  Charlie, I have come for thee!

There may come sad days of sighing
Over hopes so slowly dying,
And our hearts in secret crying :
   God of mercy, pity me !
But should sorrow hover o'er us,
May this bright hope go before us,
Always singing this sweet chorus :
   Charlie, I have come for thee !

LITTLE INJUN DICK.

Little Injun Dick
Was up to ev'ry trick,
Tho' he was but a dozen years old;
   In summer he run bare,
   Except his head of hair,
A breech cloth added when the nights got cold.

His daddy was a chief,
Also a horse thief,
And he loved whisky better than his kid;
   He had the biggest maw
   For rum you ever saw,
And many a quart into it slid.

Little Injun Dick
Found a dynamite stick
Some prospector had lost in the wood;
   And, thinking it sweet meat,
   He began at once to eat,
And said, "White man's sausage welly good."

Then home he ran with glee
To his father's teepee,
And found the old man drunk as a lord;
He had just whipped his squaw
For having too much jaw
And trying to get in the last word.

When little Dick came in
He was cussing like sin,
And the moment he set eyes on his kid,
He made a wicked kick
At poor little Dick—
'Twas the very last thing that he did.

'Twas wonderful to see
The end of that teepee,
The dust, smoke, legs, thunder and roar;
There were entrails and hair,
And ham-strings in the air,
And it rained meat for two days or more.

SUPERSTITION.

Men know but little of nature,
Or the grass on which they have trod,
And all that, of which they know nothing,
They worship and call it their god.

THE COW BOY'S WIFE.

Sweet little Maverick, go to sleep,
　Bossie cow's bell is ringing;
The moon o'er the mountain soon will peep,
　The birds have all quit singing;
Sleep while your papa is riding
　Out where the cougar is hiding,
And baby is well in the home corral,
　While the sandman sleep is bringing.

Papa is bringing the cattle home,
　Out on the mesa they're bawling;
Supper is waiting for him to come—
　Loudly the coyote is calling.
Papa is mamma's brave hero,
　Broad is his beaded sombrero,
And we need not fear the bellowing steer,
　Nor accidents befalling.

Sleep has lassoed my baby at last,
　Sweetly he smiles in his dreaming;
Tangled in slumber's lariat fast—
　Hears not the catamount screaming.
'Bove the crag's peak over yonder
　Hang storm-clouds charged with thunder,
I hear the deep roar as it echoes o'er
　The mesa, where moonlight is streaming.

Far up the crag where the moonbeams fall,
  Through the window I'm seeing
Two pumas fierce through the moonlight crawl,
  After the antelope fleeing.
Softly the night winds are blowing,
  Louder the thunder peals growing,
Sleep, baby, sleep, while the storm-clouds creep,
  The midnight storm decreeing.

Hark! in the distance the cattle bawl,
  I hear the cow boys yelling ;
And papa's voice rings above them all—
  My lonely heart is swelling.
Sometimes I sigh for the city,
  Where friends think of me in pity,
But I love the steer and the wild life here,
  And my heart with joy is welling.

FORETHOUGHT.

"Will you love me when I'm old?"
  Said the whisky to the man ;
"You'll be better then, I'm told,
  And I'll love you all I can."
"Will you love me when I'm old?
  When there's wrinkles on my brow?"
"Then I may be turned to mould,
  So I'd better drink you now."

IT IS EASY TO TALK.

It is easy to talk of your virtue
   When you have grown old and gray,
When your blood is cold and your heart is old,
   And passion has faded away;
But the young man may fall to temptation
   The maiden act indiscreet,
For the sins of youth are really, in truth,
   A something awfully sweet.

To tell how to get wealthy is easy,
   When your fortune is already made;
But the man in the yoke will think it no joke
   To make millions by his trade.
For the great world is always changing,
   Aad chances are not the same,
And the hog in most men is as great as then,
   And the shrewd have blocked ev'ry game.

It is easy to talk of wisdom,
   If you yourself have been schooled;
But the factory child who works all the while,
   By just such as you are fooled;
For you lie to them, and deceive them,
   And tell them God has made
A particular few with nothing to do,
   While millions must work at their trade.

It is easy to talk of religion,
   And speak of the mercies of God,
While you hold in your hand the fat of the land,
   Accumulated by fraud;
But the poor man, in rags and tatters,
   With his children crying for bread,
Knows very well there could be no worse hell
   Fall over his poor weary head.

THUNDER STORM ON THE ROCKIES.

The dark clouds hang o'er the mountains;
   The crags, again and again,
Seem to stab the storm clouds bosom,
   And make it roar with pain;
The lightning wickedly flashing,
   Illuminating the sky,
Seems like a terrible warning—
   The storm will conquer or die.

And midst the roar and the flashing
   'Round the rugged crag's high head,
The monstrous mountains tremble
   Like giants filled with dread;
And the lurid streaks of lightning
   Darting athwart the cloud,
And thunderbolts loud jolting
   Behind the storm-crest proud.

The heavens are filled with grandeur,
 And the thunder's mighty roar,
Seems like a voice Almighty
 And shouting from shore to shore;
And the fog banks down the canyon,
 Afloat like rivers of love,
Are drifting to the storm clouds,
 Like down from a snow-white dove.

And from the valley beholding
 The grandeur of nature's might,
I'm standing in awe and transport
 At such a majestic sight;
And I hear the great clouds roaring
 Like demons in great pain,
And the whirlwinds in the valley
 Go dancing before the rain.

And the withered vegetation
 Takes on fresh hope, I think,
And to the storm-god of nature,
 Holds out its hands for a drink.
But the storm clouds are receding,
 They seldom cross the plain,
And down in the sun-dried valley
 The flowers still cry for rain.

SONG OF THE BURRO.

I am the emblem of patience and hope,
The angel of the great Pacific slope;
Though not embellished with aesthetic grace,
I have a very remarkable face—
       I'm a burro.

Some men call me the mountain canary,
And others call me the canyon fairy,
But instead of feathers I am hairy,
And cannot warble so light and airy—
       I'm a burro.

Old poets love to sing of fairy land,
Where a little wrinkled woman with a wand,
Can order half the universe to stand;
But when you want a fairy thats got the sand,
       Take a burro.

Take me, for instance, with my sweet brown eyes,
Where you see reflected the summer skies;
Where hope and patience never, never dies;
But I sometimes give the boys a surprise,
       'Cause I'm a burro.

When they mount me in groups of three or four,
All crowded until I will hold no more,
From head to tail, as I said before,
I do sometimes scatter them on the floor—
       The rights of a burro.

Sometimes big men will sit astraddle
Of my back, without blanket or saddle,
And then make me get up and skedaddle,
With the aid of stirrups or paddle—
          Poor burro.

In the mountains rich minerals are found,
Where only a burro can tramp the ground,
And, poor little cuss, he is loaded down
With rich silver quartz and started for town—
          Poor burro.

Then he is beaten and driven along
With the sharp goad-stick or raw-hide thong;
Given no time to indulge in a song,
But he often shrieks in a voice so strong—
          Voice of a burro.

Waw-haw! waw-hee! yaw-waw, haw-he-ee-ee!
That is the old song you will hear from me,
Away up in the mountain air so free:
Waw-hee! that's me with song so free, waw-hee!
          I'm a burro.

I am the emblem of patience and hope,
The angel of the great Pacific slope;
I'm controlled by neither preacher nor pope;
If you tie me up I will chew the rope—
          I'm a burro.

THE MISER OF LOST CANYON.

It was night and the moon lit up the mountain,
And the stars like diamonds glittered in the sky;
Down in the shadows by the bubbling fountain
The poor old prospector was going to die.
For long years, without a single companion,
Old Eagle-Eyed Abner had hunted for gold;
Over the mountain trail and lonely canyon,
Through the heat of Summer and Winter's cold,
The old man had wasted his youth and manhood.
Searching for the nuggets of Indian lore;
Knowing no home but a bed in the wild wood,
Under the cedars on the moss-covered floor.

Seventy years had passed to oblivion,
And the poor old prospector was bent and gray;
He had asked himself why he should go living on,
But he found his bonanza that very same day!
Under the granite rock up in Lost Canyon
He had found it at last—it was gold, gold, gold!
And now, far away from friend and companion,
Danced with delight at what his eyes did behold.
Then down on the ground he sat all a-tremble;
Some one might hear him and be led to the spot!
His feelings no longer he could dissemble—
He was now a miser in every thought.

Carefully he hid all trace of his treasure,
Covering it up with the dead leaves and moss,
Never devising any means or measure
To extract the gold from the granite and dross.
He was rich now—this was all he required.
At last his efforts had been crowned with success;
All love, and mercy, and kindness expired,
And he even now loved his poor self much less.
A week went by, and the old man still lingered,
Eating nothing, but drinking at the fountain :
While the samples from his gold rock he fingered,
And watched the sun rise and set on the mountain.

Weaker and still weaker now the old man grew,
And at last could only crawl down for a drink :
But he kept his golden rock always in view,
And seldom or never of grim death did think.
And now it is night on the moon-lit mountain,
And the stars like diamonds glitter overhead ;
And the darksome shadows down at the fountain
Are hiding the face of the miserable dead.

Oh, the miserable death of the mountain miser !
Now lying so stiff by the side of his gold :
Still grasping his samples, but now no wiser
Than the rocks beside him in the shadows cold.
And the moon ascending shines down the canyon,
And melts the shadows from the face of the dead—
Died as he lived, without friend or companion,
Thinking of his gold until the last breath fled.

IF CHRIST WERE HERE.

If I told you of a Savior
  In a lowly stable born,
Could I tell by your behavior
  That you gave the least concern
To his welfare or his mission?
  If his parents were both poor,
Would you bow in meek submission
  Just outside the stable door?

Now, if this was in the city,
  And the parents had no cash,
Would you mingle, with your pity,
  Contempt for such lowly trash?
Would you not laugh in derision
  At the idea of a God
Meeting with such poor provision,
  In a world where prophets trod?

Would you take them into your house?
  Saying beggars, welcome here!
No; you'd cry, Off to the poor house!
  There's the pauper's proper sphere.
Likewise, if you owned the stable
  Where the unknown Jesus lay,
You'd collect some rent, if able;
  Or would drive them all away.

You can boast of loving Jesus,
   Knowing that He reigns above;
If He came as poor as Laz'rus,
   To the winds would fly your love.
To the police you'd be flying,
   With an angry, hurried tread;
In the chain gang Christ be tying,
   If He dared to ask for bread.

Even in the gilded temple,
   Christ, in rags, would dare not pray;
There's no seat for one so simple
   'Mongst the Christians of to-day.
Christ the mighty, up in glory,
   Having blessings to bestow,
Reads like quite another story,
   Than a beggar down below.

Do you think God you're deceiving?
   Do you think that Christ is blind?
Do you think this make-believing
   Teaches Christ that you are kind?
Does not Christ know ev'ry beggar
   That comes knocking at your door?
Would the God who guarded Hagar
   Overlook the worthy poor?

God's fair earth you go on fencing,
   To the best you lay a claim,
And your vile laws you're dispensing,
   To the Lord Almighty's shame.

For, on earth, Christ's greatest mission
  Was God's justice to declare;
Do you think you have permission
  To rob poor men of their share?

Do you think the loving Savior
  Has not wisely laid his plan?
Does He not see our behavior
  Shown towards our fellow man?
In the beggar you receive Him;
  In the prison He is too;
If you truly then believe Him,
  All are Christ's who come to you.

SILVER THREADS.

I love these old gray heads
  With hair of silver gray;
Their tangled silver threads,
  Bleached like the meadow hay :
They bring to me a face
  Out of the shadows deep,
And loving lines I trace,
  Like those of one asleep
Far away on the hill
  Where my dead lov'd ones lie,
And where I hope I will
  Be buried when I die.

Gray hair, like faded moss,
  Draping the wrinkled brow,
Purified from all dross—
  No bright, gay colors now.
Shroud for the buried past ;
  A rose of death for age ;
A flag of truce at last ;
  Of life's book the last page.
Dear gray hair, moist with tears
  Of children, whose small hands
Cling to it in their fears,
  And hold the silver strands.

Gray hair, you touch my heart,
  And cause my soul to chide ;
Twixt life and death you part,
  Where death and life divide.
But yet, when out of place,
  Or in the butter hid,
You bring the same disgrace
  As hair from off a "kid."
If baked within the bread,
  And swallowed by mistake,
We honor not the head
  Of she who did it bake.

Gray hair, like royal crown,
  You have your place to shine.
But, please do not fall down
  Into this soup of mine.
I love you on the head
  Where you do flourish thin,

But, on my buttered bread,
   I hate you worse than sin.
Shroud of the buried past,
   You honor any head,
But don't you get baked fast
   In gobs of sour bread.

THE LOST TROOPERS.

On the plains of Arizona,
   O'er the parch'd and burning sands,
Slowly rode the squad of troopers,
   Fighting only thirst's demands.
Days and days they saw no water,
   And their old guide had been lost,
For the sand-hills had been shifting,
   In the winds their atoms toss'd.

Now they rode on searching water,
   Horses, riders, almost dead ;
Tongues were parched and half protruding,
   And their eyes were crimson red.
Some are falling to the rearward,
   Half concluding there to die,
But their captain cheers them onward,
   And once more the brave men try.

Softly night is falling on them,
And the moon, so full and round,
Slowly rises in the Heavens,
Casts long shadows on the ground.
And they hear the water murmur
In imagination's dream,
And they often mistake shadows
In the distance for a stream.

"Water! water!" cries each trooper,
Goaded on by thirst's keen smart;
'Tis the cry of delirium,
'Tis a whisper in each heart ;
For they know that in the morning,
When the sun shall rise again,
It will add more to their terror,
Shining down upon the plain.

But, joy ! at early morning
They all hear a small bird sing,
And the old guide then assures them
They are nearing some cool spring.
"God be praised!" they see its glimmer,
And the early-rising sun
Is reflected on the water—
Horse and trooper try to run.

"Water! water!" hearts are shouting,
But the voice of all is still,
For their tongues are parched and swollen,
And they cannot speak until

They have plunged into the water—
Blessed water! clear and deep;"
And they drink it in so thankful,
Hearts so glad—for joy they weep.

Ah, that water—*poison water*!
From the copper, under ground,
It is charged with fatal poison.
"See the dead coyotes around!
They have drank this fatal water,
Then have fallen here and died!
We shall soon now all be like them!"
Cried the terror-stricken guide.

Long the fate of these brave troopers
Was a myst'ry at the post,
But each year a scouting party
Searched the desert for the lost.
And, at last, two old prospectors
This deceptive water found,
And were cautioned not to drink it,
Seeing dead men on the ground.

Horses, troopers, lying bleaching,
Faces upturned to the sun,
Their sad fate, by pencil written,
Fluttered in the hand of one:
"Take this message, who shall find us,
To my mother far-away.
Ah, please God, she may have died ere
She shall hear of this sad day.

"Touch you not this fatal water,
For by God it is accurs'd ;
It has death within its bubbles,
Oh, be tempted not by thirst.
My companions all have perished ;
I can see them where they lay :
And I'll be among their number
Ere the closing of the day."

MORAL.

There's a desert called "Ambition,"
Where men struggle hard for gain ;
Where the barren, parch'd condition
Shows that mercy cannot reign :
Where a pool of gold is standing,
So inviting to our thirst,
And our avarice demanding
More and more, until we burst.

All around this pool are lying
Bodies rotting in the sun,
And among them are the dying,
Who a poisoned drink have won ;
For the water, impregnated
With that poison—"Love of Gold,"
Makes the drinker, dissipated,
Die of agonies untold.

SMOTHERED THOUGHTS.

I have thoughts so strange and knowing
    In my heart,
And their numbers keep on growing—
    Can't depart.
Tho' the cage is never stout,
Still these thought-birds come not out,
For there's prejudice about,
And there's superstition showing
    Her long dart.

Could I but send these birds adrift,
    Like the lark,
They might create a little rift
    In the dark;
But grim prejudice would fall
On each thought-bird, and they'd all
Become smothered in the brawl,
And the world reject the gift
    From the start.

So I'll cage these thoughts securely,
    And I'll try
To think thoughts like the purely:
    Even I
Will not offend the owls,
Who look on me with scowls,
And stir up savage growls
From all those who think so surely
    That I lie.

And I'll try, with coming age,
That which smothers
These thought-birds in their cage,
     And no others
Of these thought-birds be getting,
And keep them there a fretting,
Behind this cruel netting,
          Like their brothers.

Oh, this world is but a cage
     To the mind
That would step beyond the age.
     And mankind,
In a blinded, struggling crowd,
Where the humble and the proud,
Are crying, long and loud,
          Get behind!

Trust the preachers, politicians,
     False and true,
And let these modern magicians
     Think for you:
Let them always take the lead,
Let them gauge your time and speed,
Follow blindly, then, indeed,
          You will do.

If they say the world is flat,
     Say so, too.
Galileo found out that—
     So will you.

If they say, all men who doubt
Do not know what they're about,
Say so, too.   If not right out,
    Say "um—hoo."

THE CLIFF DWELLERS.

In the giant sand rock canyon
    Where the stunted cedars grow,
And the sunshine in abandon
    Parches dry the earth below ;
Far beyond the Mount La Plata,
    In the lowei Mancos pass,
Where the ancient Soangetaha
    Lov'd the dusky mountain lass.

From the upper snow clad Mesas,
    When the snows begin to thaw,
There's a thousand Minnehahas
    Pouring down the rocky draw ;
Rushing off to meet the river,
    By some subtle power drawn,
Where the water flows forever
    Roughly down the swift San Juan.

Here are traces of a nation,
    Dead to mem'ry long ago ;
But from lofty elevation,
    Where the stunted cedars grow,

There are castles, long since passing
   Into ruin, and the dust
On the rocky floors amassing,
   Slowly ages did adjust.

No one knows their ancient story,
   And the silence reigning here,
Whispers nothing of their glory,
   Nothing of their hopes or fear ;
But some bones of human creatures,
   Yellow with their age and rust,
Skull-bones showing human features,
   Have been found among the dust.

Here we know in long dead ages
   Hearts did ache and souls did love,
Here the youths and older sages
   Watched fair Luna shine above.
Here the mother nursed her baby,
   Hugged it to her dusky breast,
Sang some woodland ditty, maybe,
   Until it had sank to rest.

Now the silence, deep and painful,
   Fills your soul with dreadful awe,
And the raven's voice disdainful
   Rasps your ear with his shrill "caw."
Standing where this nation perished,
   Knowing nothing of their strife—
For the secrets their hearts cherished
   Pass'd away with their strange life.

How your soul is filled with wonder,
  And you wish you could be told
How long since the crash of thunder
  Shook their bodies into mould.
Ah, perhaps 'twas long ere Moses
  Brought the plagues to Pharoah's land,
This dead valley bloomed like roses,
  Tilled by a strange human hand.

Oh, I never dreamed in childhood,
  In my home so far away,
There would come a time when I would
  Stand where ages of decay
Melts the castles of a nation,
  Crumbles into mouldering dust,
And find in the ruination
  Crumbling skulls of yellow dust.

This poor skull between my fingers,
  Cimmerian darkness now
In each eyeless socket lingers—
  All is silence, and the brow,
Once filled with life's strange mystery,
  Now for ages in repose—
How I long to know the hist'ry
  None but the Almighty knows.

YOU AND I TOGETHER.

Down life's curious river we float,
　You and I together;
Each passenger in his little boat,
　You and I together;
In some places the channel is deep,
With plenty of room for each other's sweep;
While in other places great rocks sleep,
And their rough heads near the surface peep,
　And stormy is the weather.

Shall we then crowd our neighbor ashore?
　You and I together;
Wrecking his boat and breaking his oar?
　You and I together;
Shall we crowd him upon the rough rocks,
Where the human boat receives great shocks,
And the rushing waves his struggle mocks,
And famine grim the whole year stalks,
　Searching for our brother?

Are we brothers, or are we not?
　You and I together;
Should we be sharing each other's lot?
　You and I together;
Shall we assist when storm clouds fall,
And darkness settles down like a pall?
Or run away when our neighbors call—
Each one for himself and the devil for all;
　Is this your motto, brother?

Oh, why not lash together each boat?
   You and I together;
Out in the current where all can float?
   You and I together;
Oh, why not lend an oar, or a sail,
To our poor brother about to fail?
Why stop our ears to his bitter wail,
And let him sink in our own ship's trail!
   Are we so heartless, brother?

Great God, in mercy pity our greed!
   You and I together;
And help us heal the hearts that bleed,
   You and I together;
Let us tow our weak brother along
Down the stream, and cheer him with song,
Pull his frail boat from out among
The cruel rocks, where the fierce sharks throng
   And try to eat our brother.

Oh, life is only a little trip!
   You and I together;
And the same God made each little ship,
   You and I together;
And He launched us all upon this stream,
And made our sails of the bright sunbeam;
And there is room for all, but it seems
We are all too full of greedy schemes,
   And try to sink our brother.

LEFT BEHIND.

"Go back," he said to the mongrel cur,
When he made an attempt to follow;
And the dog laid down by the cabin door
And licked his paws, while his heart was sore,
And watched his master passing o'er
The desert sands, hot and mellow.

This happened out on the West frontier,
On the desert of Colorado.
The man was a man without love or fear,
Who had seen, perhaps, his fiftieth year,
Whose eyes ne'er shed a pitying tear—
He'd the heart of a desperado.

His mission now was to homestead land
On the desert so dry and dreary.
His cabin he built with his own strong hand,
A rough board shed on the desert sand,
And water he brought from the river Grand,
And he lived with his dog quite cheery.

Now he is going to the far-off town
On his broncho so lean and bony;
And he cast behind one angry frown
At the cringing dog, now lying down,
Then cantered away towards the town
On his lean and sad-eyed pony.

A week pass'd by. The dog still lay
Where his cruel master had left him ;
Looking and longing, day after day,
Down the trail where his master rode away,
Over the dry sand parched and gray,
And of his presence bereft him.

Ah, do you think, had the poor dog known
How his master in town was drinking—
Would he have lain so patiently down,
With all that painful silence around,
Dying of thirst, and not of a wound ?—
'Twould have been all the same, I'm thinking.

"To-morrow he'll come," the dog would say,
"I will wait until to-morrow."
The night passed on. The morning gray
Ushered in one more dreary day,
And the poor dog could not go away,
But waited, and waited in sorrow.

Is there a god to tradition known
More faithful to obedience proving?
Dying of hunger, and all alone ;
Dying without a tear or a groan ;
Greater faith by man was never shown :
The equal of gods in loving.

"To-morrow he'll come," the dog did sigh,
As darkness obscured the view ;
But in the night grim death stalked by,

And stilled his heart, and glazed each eye.
A martyr to love that dog did die—
Could a god be more faithful and true?

His life went out on the desert breath—
Oh, where did his spirit go?
Could there die a man with stronger faith?
And is there not, above or beneath,
Some record kept of this noble death?
And a future reward also?

Greater love than this never was known,
A love that is strong in death's sorrow.
Dying for love's sake, without a moan,
For the life he loved giving his own—
Will this for his master's sins atone
In death's mysterious to-morrow?

When the wretched man came back at last
He found the poor dog laying
Beside the door, with his eyes closed fast;
Heart stilled by that silent hand which pass'd;
And the wretched man stood there aghast,
Too guilty even for praying.

Out of all this mystery, I know,
We are promised a salvation.
But we are so thoughtless here below,
So painfully cruel as we go
Through this wicked world, to and fro,
Filling it with damnation.

LITTLE MAVERICK.

It was born in bleak November,
　　When the snow began to fly;
'Twas a meek-eyed, little bull calf,
　　With the saddest, dreary cry;
And 'twould wag it's tail at strangers
　　While they sauntered slowly by.

But the weather growing colder
　　Made the little critter jump,
And the hair stood out like bristles
　　All over its little rump;
But, in milking its old mother,
　　It did not forget to bump.

But the louse came in mid-winter
　　To prospect upon that calf;
Chewed the hair off in great patches,
　　In a way to make you laugh;
Soon his tail would hardly wiggle,
　　While his daily milk he'd quaff.

In the early, balmy springtime
　　When the shadflies filled the air,
All unbranded and unchristened,
　　And without a doctor there,
This poor calf, so lean and lousy,
　　Gently climbed the golden stair.

Now, the question here uprises:
  Who this Maverick will own
In the pasture fields of Eden,
  Where it's spirit now has flown?
For it passed away unbranded,
  Climbed the golden stair alone.

Will it find the summer ranges
  Full of cattle men have slain?
Waiting there to greet their butchers   ·
  And be branded then again?
Will they brand this calf in Eden
  E're a stall it can obtain?

DREAMING OF HOME.

Near the graveyard on the Mesa,
  Where the sun forever shines,
Glist'ning on the cold, white tombstones,
  Brought from far-off marble mines ;
There I often sit when lonely,
  Near the city of the dead,
While the dreams of home and childhood
  Softly come into my head.

Down the road so long and dusty,
  Weary horsemen come and go ;
Each one wears a broad sombrero,
  But there's scarcely one I know.

Mexicans so dark and swarthy,
  Riding ponies lean as death,
Cowboys dashing by so madly,
  Horse and man both out of breath.

I can look across the river,
  Far beyond the ragged town,
Out among the hills of 'dobe,
  Where no thing of life is found,
But a bunch of stunted greasewood,
  Growing in the 'dobe clay,
And small bunches of coarse salt sage,
  Faded out like sun-dried hay.

All the earth seems parch'd and dreary,
  No green hills to rest the eye;
God in Heaven! must I linger
  In this dreary place and die?
Then I dream of a fair valley
  Where Bald Eagle mountains stand,
And where flows the Susquehanna
  Softly through that far-off land?

Sometimes on the mesa dreaming,
  Dreams I long and long to tell,
Far away my heart goes yearning
  For the water in the well,
At the dear old home of childhood,
  'Mong the everlasting hills,
Where I used to sit in summer
  List'ning to the whip-poor-wills.

And sometimes my wife beside me
  Wonders why I am so still,
Looking o'er the lifeless desert
  Out toward the 'dobe hill ;
And sometimes sad tears of longing
  On my lashes she espies,
But she thinks I look too eager,
  And the sunlight hurts my eyes.

There are many poor hearts aching
  On this dry Pacific slope,
Toiling in the burning sun rays,
  Cheered alone by this one hope :
That some day the wheel of fortune,
  In its slow, uncertain turn,
May enable them to journey
  Back to where their poor hearts yearn.

But each week, out on the Mesa,
  To the graveyard at this place,
Slowly moves the hearse and coffin,
  Dragging out a cold, white face ;
Some poor heart has ceased its yearning,
  And the dreams of hope have fled ;
None but God will know the story
  Of the poor, heart-broken dead.

OBLIVION.

Deep in a Colorado canyon—
  So the story goes—
  Two Spaniards bold,
  Prospecting for gold,
    Near where a small creek flows,
Heard the roar of a mighty storm above,
  And the waters rushing,
  And the mine was filled,
  The miners killed,
    By the great flushing.

Great rocks rolled and filled up the canyon,
  And the prospect hole
  Was hidden from sight,
  In the storm's great might.
    Now the waters roll
And tumble forever above them,
  And none but God knows
  Each horrified face,
  In this hiding place,
    Where they now repose.

And the coyotes howling above them,
  And the eagle's call,
  And the ravens, high
  In the azure sky,
    While the cougars crawl

Over the rocks which conceal this tomb
Where the miners fell.
Oblivion deep—
Oblivious sleep!
None their story tell.

And the howling winds of winter,
And falling snow;
Then comes balmy spring,
The summer birds sing—
They all come and go:
But under the rocks they are lying,
Those men so clever;
Oblivion deep,
Oblivious sleep—
Sleep on forever!

But how much better will be my fate?
Even tho' my tomb
Is bathed with tears
Of loved ones, for years.
There still is gloom;
And, tho' my story is known to men,
How long will it be
Until none but God
Knows where the sod
Covers up poor me?

Oblivion! 'tis only to be
Forgotten by all.
Whether low or deep
The place where we sleep—
Whether great or small—

Soon, soon will this great oblivion
All trace dissever :
Sleep on, thou sleeper !
The shadows grow deeper ;
Sleep on forever !

O-NA-WEE-TA.

NOTE.—Many years ago there was a battle fought in Arizona between United States troops and a band of Indian cattle thieves, in which many poor soldiers were killed. One poor fellow was wounded very badly, but he clung to his horse, and was carried many miles from the place before he fell from his saddle. He landed in a dense thicket of manzanita brush, where he was found by an Indian maiden, who nursed him, and even shot and wounded her old father in defense of the poor fellow. The young couple were afterwards married, and also forgiven by the fierce old warrior.

Down where the water flows,
    Soft music purling,
Smoke from the teepee rose,
    In the zephyrs whirling;
Songs of the summer birds
    In the manzanita,
Mingle with the gentle words
    Of O-na-wee-ta.

Pride of the warrior's eye,
    Fierce old Wah-hee-tah,
Eyes like the midnight sky,
    Sweet O-na-wee-ta :

Singing like a summer bird
  In the manzanita,
Sweeter voice was never heard
  Than O-na-wee-ta's.

Out in the chaparral
  Lay a wounded soldier;
Found at last where he fell
  By a fair beholder:
Hunting for the timid hare
  In the manzanita,
She found the soldier there—
  Sweet O-na-wee-ta.

Kindly she dressed his sores,
  Took sweet broth to him,
In his wounds some ointment pours,
  Gently did woo him.
Father followed her one day—
  Fierce old Wah-hee-tah—
Found where the soldier lay
  In the manzanita.

Fiercely he draws his knife,
  Eyes shine with murder;
Daughter cries, "Spare his life!"
  But he never heard her:
Soon then a pistol flash'd
  In the manzanita,
Through his arm a bullet crash'd—
  Brave O-na-wee-ta!

"Touch not the sick pale-face!
I stand above him;
Tho' he's not of my race,
Father, I love him!
'Twas the Great Spirit led me
To the manzanita,
And soon he'll wedded be
To his O-na-wee-ta."

Loudly the warrior curs'd,
Fierce old Wah-hee-tah;
For revenge his heart did thirst
On O-na-wee-ta;
But soon he did relent,
Fierce old Wah-hee-tah:
There's a marriage in the tent—
Happy O-na-wee-ta!

MY CHURCH.

The religion I want is mercy,
Love, charity, and justice for all;
A church that will welcome the lowly,
And stoop to pick up those who fall.
But a faith that asks God for mercy,
In a world where laboring men call
In vain for a share of God's blessings,
For shame! 'Tis no religion at all.

ALONE BY THE RIVER.

The day was so dreary and sober,
   The leaves had turned yellow and sere,
It was in melancholy October,
   The saddest, sad month of the year—
   The lonesomest month of the year :
Death comes to nature to disrobe her,
   To strip her boughs naked and bare,
And the trees stand solemn and sober,
   Like images standing in prayer.

In silence I walk by the river,
   That swift flowing river—the Grand,
Where the sun on the wavelets shiver,
   As they tumble ashore on the sand—
   Ashore on the gold-bearing sand :
And the glint of the sunbeams quiver
   On the pebbles reflecting their rays,
But my thoughts are ever and ever
   Flowing back to my childhood days.

Oh, why am I here by this river—
   Here walking and dreaming alone ?
And why do I tremble and shiver,
   And my willing exile bemoan—
   My melancholy exile bemoan?
Oh, why do these yellow leaves falling
   From the cottonwood trees on the shore,
Remind me of childhood friends calling,
   But drowned by the river's deep roar?

Why can I not search for bright pebbles
    As I walk on the beach of the Grand?
And why are my thoughts such great rebels?
    Going back to that far-off land—
    That dear, old, cherished far-off land.
These shadows on the swift river dancing,
    Are they the ghosts of my lov'd ones dead?
For something my heart is entrancing,
    And this loneliness fills me with dread.

Right here on this sand where I'm walking
    The Indians in past years have trod;
They have listened to the Grand river talking,
    For the voice of the water was God—
    The murmuring water was God:
While out on the Mesa the jaguar
    And coyote for venison strove,
And the beautiful, blood-thirsty cougar
    Looked down from the crag's peak above.

But now, in this month of October,
    There's silence and sadness around,
And the trees, standing silent and sober,
    Are dropping their leaves on the ground—
    The alkali-salt-covered ground:
And the Indians have all cross'd the river,
    And gave to the white man their land,
And the water has wash'd out forever
    Their tracks from the soft yielding sand.

And those of that tribe now still living
  May be somewhere walking alone :
And, instead of heartfelt thanksgiving,
  Their dreary, forced exile bemoan—
  Their long, compelled exile bemoan :
And the ghosts of the men fierce and sober
  Who fought by the side of Ouray,
May have come, like the frosts of October,
  To carry some new life away.

Thus dreaming I walk by the river,
  The canyon-walled river—the Grand,
And I wonder, so sadly, if ever
  I'll walk in that far-off, dear land?
  'Mongst the hills of that far-off land :
And I gaze in the water, so sober,
  While I dig with my heel in the sand,
And I wonder if ever October
  Was so sad in that far-off land.

CASTING BREAD.

Cast your bread upon the hungry,
  Not on water, as 'tis said,
And they'll return to you quite often—
  Those that hunger, not the bread.
Bread that's cast upon the water
  Never will return again ;
For it soon dissolves to batter,
  Or in sour wads remain.

A SLIGHT MISTAKE.

On the battle field of Gettysburg a wounded soldier lay;
A cannon ball had come along and torn his leg away.
A scarred old veteran came that way, cheering himself with
   songs,
A genuine old soldier boy whose hair stood out in prongs.
"Oh carry me from this dreadful place!" the wounded
   soldier moaned;
The smoky comrade picked him up and lazily he groaned.
With the wounded soldier on his back he held him by each
   hand,
And, ev'ry step, the poor man's blood stream'd down and
   stained the sand.

"Where are you hurt?" the comrade ask'd the wounded
   man aloft.
"A cannon ball," he made reply, "has torn my right leg
   off."
"An' so it is your laig, comrade," the soldier soothing said.
And just then came a cannon ball and took also the head.
But the wounded soldier scarcely kicked, so sudden was
   the blow;
And, death thus coming like a flash, his comrade did not
   know,
But went jogging from the battle field, toting his load
   along;
Never thinking of blood or death, but humming low a
   song.

But a captain met him by and by, who closely scanned his
    load;
And when he saw the headless trunk, said, "Drop it in
    the road!
This man is dead as dead can be—his head is shot clean
    off!"
The comrade dropped his heavy load and gave an angry
    cough.
"Wal, dod durn him, when I picked him up, as sure as
    my name's Waig,
He told me he was wounded bad, but said it was his leg!

BEDTIME.

Bedtime, and I lay me down to sleep,
    While the moon shines brightly overhead;
And the shadows lengthen out and creep
    In through the window upon my bed:
But before I sleep I take a peep
    Into the past, where my years have fled.

I see a dark room with rafters bare,
    And three small beds in the shadows deep;
And I know the little sleepers there,
    So very weary and fast asleep.
And over the hill the whip-poor-will
    Echoes the chirp of the little "knee-deep."

Those happy nights of the long ago!
　When three little brothers lay awake,
Counting the rain drops falling slow,
　Laughing loud at each other's mistake;
And the cricket's call in the chimney wall
　Such doleful music all night does make.

Bedtime—happiest hour of all
　To the weary man going to rest,
With a conscience clear to rest I fall,
　So like a child on its mother's breast;
And while I sleep, the long shadows creep
　Over my face from the moon-lit west.

Bedtime—oh! when the last night shall come,
　And the shadows dark around me fall,
And the gloom of death hangs o'er my home,
　And I faintly hear my loved ones call;
Oh! may I dream, and death but seem
　A child-like slumber for us all.

THERE IS NO FRIENDSHIP.

There is no such thing as friendship.
　I learned this truth of late;
To the millions we are indifferent,
　While a few we love—and hate.

THE CURSE OF COLORADO.

There's a curse on Colorado,
  There's a Hell at Cripple Creek,
Where the golden Eldorado
  Grows more wicked every week ;
Where the virgin soil is tainted
    With the murder'd strikers' blood,
And on ev'ry face is painted :
    I am making gold my god.

There are many lone graves hidden
  In the woods, beyond Bull Hill,
Where deputies have ridden,
    Who were sworn to slay and kill ;
And the thunders cannot waken
    Those who sleep beneath the sod,
But each night some life is taken
    In this place where gold is god.

Here the lights all night are burning,
  And the game is always on,
And bad men to demons turning,
    Through the gold they lost or won ;
Here the harlots, thieves and devils,
    Have their coarse hands stained with blood,
And a thousand other evils
    Reign where gold alone is god.

One would think the elevation,
  (Ten thousand feet above the sea,)
Would bring it in close relation
  To the God of Galilee ;
But the sun, from its position,
  Ev'ry morning finds new blood
Staining this pocket edition
  Of Hell, where gold reigns as god.

THE ACCURSED CITIES.

Accursed cities! say Nature's laws;
Where streets stand gaping like mighty jaws,
And all the glittering scenes within
Are hiding some dark and bestial sin,
And luring strangers therein to walk,
By rash promises and idle talk.
Too soon those buildings become a wall,
To drown the groans and dying call
Of the poor, polluted human beast,
Who is forced on plunder there to feast;
And where virtue is as little known
As saints in hades, and the moan
Of poverty, and hunger, and death,
Mingle with the drunken dancer's breath.

Accursed cities! say honest priests,
Who see their brothers in sinful feasts;
For the minister who reads the signs

On faces where intemperance reigns,
Knows of the dark hell raging within
The poor soul, drunken to drown its sin.
And each pinched face seen on the street,
And all the naked, shivering feet,
And all the rags and thread-bare clothes,
And every trace of human woes,
Speak of poverty and sore distress
In words which law cannot suppress,
Even tho' the rich would wish it done,
And imprison ev'ry pauper's son.

Accursed cities! the rivers say,
Where foul sewers empty ev'ry day,
And the filth of millions stain the streams,
Which were created pure as dreams.
Accursed cities! whisper the winds,
Coming laden with the scent of pines:
But, when passing through the filthy towns,
Sobbing and sighing with many frowns,
Millions of germs they carry away,
To spread disease for many a day;
And the smell of filth, and smoke, and gas,
Are carried over the tender grass;
And Nature shrinks from the filthy scent,
Saying, Accursed cities! you need repent.

Give me the desert, with barren sand,
With desolation on ev'ry hand,
With its dreaded silence, bleaching bones,
Where the winds sigh in such mournful tones,

And all is desolation and waste,
And even the winds of alkali taste,
And the sun shines down with furnace heat,
And nowhere grows a spear to eat,—
Give me this, instead of wicked towns,
Where oppression forever abounds;
Where men feast on their neighbor's toil,
And, in the rush and fierce turmoil,
The poor are trampled to the ground,
And God's mercy is but seldom found.

Accursed cities! where congregate
Those who by plunder make themselves great;
The gay and gaudy aristocrat,
The tyrant and the autocrat,
The money-lender, rent-collector,
Sweat-shop owner and slave-director,
Courtesan, the gambler and thug,
The libertine with pitfalls dug;
And all those who do not honest toil,
But live on the honey and the oil
Of all the world's best products, and then
Are posing as fine gentlemen.
Accursed cities! ruination
Of our boasted civilization.

And I, too—writer of these lines,
Knowing how well hypocrisy shines;
Knowing how the rich, by usury,
Force the poor into penury;
Knowing how the churches hide the men

Who rob the poor, then come back again
And on the altar some plunder lay;
And kneeling before their God, do pray
That He may bless the suffering poor,
And make their sinful souls quite pure.
And the preachers, looking on these men,
Accepting their gold, and knowing when
And where they get it, as well as you,
I say, Oh, accursed cities! too.

DON'T FORGET YOUR MOTHER.

Last week brought a pleading letter
    From a mother whom I know,
Asking if I'd seen her Edward,
    Who had left her long ago.
"He was in your town, they tell me,
    When the railroad strike was on ;
Have you met, among the strangers,
    Edward, my proud, dashing son?

"Five long years ago he left me,
    Just because I did object
To his going with some young men
    Whom I never could respect.
And he cursed me in his anger,
    Fiercely slammed the door behind,
But if I could only see him,
    I would treat him, oh, so kind!

"In my dreams I see my Edward,
 And I hear him call for me,
And at times I dream of sitting
 With my Edward on my knee.
If he knew how I was yearning
 Just to see him once again,
He would hasten to his mother,
 And would cure this great heart pain."

Tell me, mothers, could I tell her,
 Form the words with pen or tongue,
That the son she loved so dearly
 For horse stealing had been hung?
Could I tell her that, through gambling,
 He had often killed for gain,
That he was a drunken demon,
 Worse, far worse, than bloody Cain?

All I did was simply tell her
 That her son had gone away,
And expressed a hope that they would
 Meet again some happy day.
I have noticed, in most cases,
 And it should be set to song,
When a boy forgets his mother,
 There is always something wrong.

Boys may go the wide world over,
 Seeking wealth with all their might,
If their hearts are true and loving,
 They will not forget to write;

But when days are spent in gambling,
  Nights in drinking and in song,
When the boy forgets his mother,
  Mother knows there's something wrong.

THE OLD STONE FENCE.

The old stone fence near the corn shed,
  Where the chipmonks hid their corn,
Where the wasp and wicked hornet
  With their nests the stones adorn ;
Where the tom-cat sat to listen,
  Watching for the timid mouse :
How his cruel eyes would glisten
  When he turned towards the house.

Father built the fence one Summer
  To inclose the orchard trees ;
It was cheaper, far, than lumber,
  And would last eternities.
And beside it grew the thistle,
  Briar-bushes, and the thorn,
Where the Summer birds would whistle
  So merrily night and morn.

On the fence I have been sitting
  When the bars were opened wide,
For the cows would leave off picking,
  And no longer would abide

In the field, among the bushes,
  Where the thorns and thistles grew,
But each critter quits, and rushes
  To the gap, and gazes through.

Longing for the grass beyond there,
  Growing 'mongst the orchard trees.
There they stand all day and wonder
  Why they can't go where they please :
Exactly like the human creature,
  Looking at the legal wall
Which surrounds the gifts of nature,
  Given for the use of all.

How like cattle we are standing—
  We, the toilers, and the poor,
By the open gap, demanding
  We shall be fenced out no more.
But the gap is watched by giants :
  Oppressors, lawyers, judges, slaves,
Soldiers, menials, and tyrants,
  And 'tis money buys these braves.

And the stone wall near the corn shed
  Father built around the trees,
Had its wasp and wicked hornet,
  And the festive bumble bees ;
And, like lawyers, they are lying
  For a victim near their nest ;
Just so soon as one they're spying
  There's commotion and unrest.

Ah, how often in the bosom
    Of my trousers I have found
Feeling so unearthly gruesome
    That, with one, great, mighty bound,
I have bounded from the stone wall,
    Like a thief pursued by law,
And the mighty, awful shrill squall
    Filled the bell-cow's heart with awe.

Thus the walls of law and bowlders
    For protection were created,
But the careless, blind beholders
    Know not these walls are related :
But they're both chock full of leeches,
    And scorpions, wasps, and bees,
And they'll bite clear through your breeches,
    And just prod you at their ease.

GOD NEVER WILLED IT SO.

A million dollar church for God,
    Damp cellars for poor labor,
Carpets where the priests have trod,
    Cold stone floors for our neighbor.
God has never willed it so,
    By precept or by fable ;
When sending Jesus Christ below
    He chose for Him a stable.

THE SHEEP HERDER.

Out upon the dreary mesa,
  On the 'dobe plains so bare,
I first met poor Casimero,
  Herding sheep in silence there;
For the upper range was buried
  Deep beneath the ice and snow,
And the bleating sheep were hurried
  To the barren plains below.

All day long in silence brooding,
  As he walked among the sheep,
Watching them the plains denuding,
  Walked he dreaming, half asleep.
He 'd not learned the art of reading,
  And his world was very small,
And the flock he now was leading
  Was to him his world and all.

Casimero loved a maiden,
  Senorita Corrillo,
And his thoughts were ever laden
  With sweet dreams of Mexico.
And the silence helped his dreaming
  As he walked among the sheep,
Starting at the raven's screaming,
  Like a child disturbed in sleep.

One day o'er the plains came riding
  On a broncho's weary back,
With a broad sombrero hiding
  Eyes like summer midnight black;
Said he: "Is this Casimero,
  Of Chihuahua, Mexico?"
And his eyes looked on our hero
  With a yearning love-lit glow.

Started he, and almost fainted,
  For the accent of that voice
To his ears was long acquainted,
  And his heart stops to rejoice.
Wide he holds his arms, and crying:
  "Senorita Corrillo!"
And into his strong arms flying
  Leaps the maid of Mexico.

THE WISE BOY.

There's the bad boy, and the glad boy,
And the boy with his trousers torn,
The ready boy, the steady boy,
And the boy who is all forlorn ;
But the boy who is bound to succeed in life,
Wear starched shirt and stand-up collar,
Is the boy who knows, by the flush on his nose,
When its best to strike dad for a dollar.

THE STRANGER.

What is life? and who am I?
   What are these strange things one sees?
Tho' I try, and try, and try,
   Conscience will not rest at ease.

All around strange faiths and creeds,
   All around I hear men pray;
Shaking in the wind like weeds
   On a dreary autumn day.

Men are pointing overhead
   To the place where great stars shine,
Saying it is where the dead
   Wafted are by laws divine.

This world seems so very cold
   That without love one would freeze;
Yet my host I ne'er behold,
   And I feel not at my ease.

And sometimes I feel adrift
   On some mysterious sea:
Clouds of gloom without a rift
   Seem to hover over me.

Through this world I daily roam,
   Like a captive, tho' I'm free;
Feel a stranger in my home,
   Watched by eyes I cannot see.

All the works of ages do
  Seem to tell me I am small—
That some ruling power, too,
  Watches sternly over all.

PLEADING EYES.

Eyes of pale blue, meek and pleading,
  Little faces looking old,
Little bare feet chapped and bleeding,
  Little bodies pinched with cold;
I was startled by their knocking
  Ere I opened up my door,
For I had been sitting, rocking,
  With my eyes upon the floor.

Two wee little boys were standing
  Just outside the parlor door,
And the eldest one demanding:
  "Do you ever help the poor?
Would you like to buy some honey?
  We have nice pound boxes here;
And our mamma needs the money—
  Papa is much worse this year.

"Papa he has got consumption,
  Sits all day among the trees,
Seldom stops to get a luncheon,
  For he works among the bees;

And we try to sell the honey—
    Little brother Tom and me,
Giving mamma all the money,
    And it helps her much, you see.

" We are only four now, mister—
    Tom and Jamie, me and Clyde;
For we buried little sister
    In the winter, when she died."
Looking in those little faces,
    Seeing eyes a-pleading so,
There I seemed to see the traces
    Of my own self, years ago.

When I used to gather berries,
    Peddle them from door to door—
Ah, great God! how fast life hurries
    Burdens on the struggling poor.
Pale blue eyes look up so pleading,
    Set in faces looking old.
For you my poor heart is bleeding,
    For I know your life is cold.

Oh, there's such a tender feeling
    In my bosom pulls and sways,
Mem'ry at my feet is kneeling,
    Pointing back to far-off days;
And these little pleading faces
    Bring back thoughts of former years,
And, in speaking, there are traces
    In my voice of pensive tears.

NOVEMBER.

Cold, cheerless month of November,
   When clouds are so somber and gray;
They bring back always to mem'ry
   The shadows of joys pass'd away.
I sit looking into the fire,
   While shadows dance over the floor,
And bleak winds outside flowing higher,
   And searching the world for God's poor.

Just hear it? Shrieking and howling,
   And threaten to break down the door.
It seems I can hear it growling:
   "I'm after God's miserable poo-o-o-r!"
See it lash the trees into furies,
   Dash the water high on the shore,
While shrieking, howling, it hurries
   In search of God's miserable poor.

"What have they done, these poor people!"
   The chimney-top asks of the wind,
As it rushes past the church steeple,
   With dead leaves trailing behind.
"Are you the poor people's keeper?
   If I freeze them, what is it to you?"
And the wind's hard voice sounds deeper
   As it hurried by with a "woo-oo-o-o!"

"Ah, the poor people have no keeper!"
Said the chimney-top with a sigh;
"And justice is such a sound sleeper—
He sleeps while the poor people die.
And I must see the world suffer,
And treat the affair as a joke;
Just like the millionaire duffer—
Stand back and do nothing but smoke."

But the wind blew saucy as ever
Around the chimney so mute,
Even reaching down so clever
And grabbing a handful of soot,
And went on shrieking and howling
And trying at each cottage door,
Then off again, wickedly growling:
"The poo-o-o-r, the miserable poo-o-o-r!"

I sit by the fire and shiver
When I hear the wind's cruel voice,
And wonder why the Good Giver
Allows the cold wind to rejoice.
If the rich would only remember,
And go searching from door to door,
Along with the winds of November,
And temper the winds for the poor!

FLOWERS MY MOTHER LOVED.

Last night upon my pillow dreaming
　　Of scenes so old,
Sweet visions of the past came streaming,
　　Like the old stories told.
One vision lingered there for hours;
　　My heart was moved;
For then I saw the dear old flowers,
　　Flowers that my mother loved.

All 'round the flower bed I wandered,
　　Like when a boy,
Where long ago the days I squandered,
　　Each hour fill'd with joy.
And there again I saw my mother,
　　From death removed;
And once again we bent together
　　Over the flowers she loved.

Those flowers that are so ungainly
　　And out of date,
I see them once again so plainly
　　Down at the old garden gate:
There's dahlias, and poppies, and locust,
　　And yellow rose,
Hollyhocks, marigolds, and crocus,
　　Down where the sweet pink grows.

There's the tiger-lily, and belle-flower,
    In red and blue;
Tulips, larkspurs, the snow-drop bower,
    Bright in the morning dew :
Morning-glories, sweet pansy faces,
    Sent from above ;
Clover blossoms in the odd places—
    Flowers of my mother's love.

And there was the daffodil blooming
    Like as of old,
And little bach'lor buttons looming
    Like little stars of gold.
There were blue-flags, and lilacs bending
    Where sweet peas roved,
And the sweet shrubs their fragrance blend-
      ing
    With the flowers my mother loved.

And living thus again with mother,
    Holding her hand,
And seeing once again my brother,
    Oh, such a dream is grand !
But soon the vision fades in waking,
    Gone is all joy ;
I weep as tho' my heart is breaking,
    Just like a home-sick boy.

THE WEARY WANDERER.

Back in the dear old homestead
  Among the orchard trees,
Before I had any friends dead,
  And the lightest Summer breeze
Was not so light and jolly
  As that boyish heart of mine,
And no thought of melancholy
  Could cause me to repine.

But all day long went dreaming
  Among the orchard trees,
Where light through the leaves came streaming
  As they danced in the Summer breeze.
But, after awhile, I tired
  Of living always at home,
And more and more desired
  A few brief years to roam.

I dreamed of towns and cities,
  Of countries far away,
And all my songs and ditties,
  As I worked among the hay,
Were about the tramp and rover
  Who roam the land and sea ;
And I wish'd my boyhood over,
  And I a tramp could be.

I pictured the broadest river
    Where steamboats come and go,
Where waves in moonlight shiver,
    And the world is all aglow
With wealth, and pride, and treasure,
    And the heart of man is free ;
And I thought, O, Lord ! such pleasure
    Would be a Heaven to me !

But now I'm sadly dreaming
    Of that home among the trees,
Where sunlight now is streaming
    Among the dancing leaves ;
And I'm tired, oh, and weary !
    And, if I could only see
That old home, once so dreary,
    How happy I would be !

For the world, with all its treasures,
    With all its rivers wide,
Can never bring the pleasures
    Of that dear old fireside.
Oh, for the dear old faces
    Which never again I'll see !
Above all other places,
    Is that dear old home to me.

WHO SPOILED THE POET.

Poets write gaily of flowers,
　　And slobber and simper of love;
They write of the birds by the hours,
　　Sing wild of the stars up above:
They call it imagination,
　　Or the vivid flight of true thought;
It would be low degradation
　　To write of the kettle or pot.

To set the angels to chiming,
　　Is the true poetical twirl—
There's nothing at all that's rhyming
　　In the name of a working girl.
To write of creatures titanic,
　　Makes heroic verses, I'm sure,
And praise to the name satanic,
　　Is better than lauding the poor.

They write of Kings and Princes,
　　Their trials, their hopes, and their pride;
You ought to see how one winces
　　To write of the beggar who died.
I'm sick of the modern poet,
　　I'm sick of the old masters, too;
They're hypocrites, and you know it—
　　If you don't, then I'm sick of you.

Why sing all the time of Heaven?
  Forgetting the crude things below.
Are eagles to music given
  Far more than the raven or crow?
The lofty peak of the mountain -
  Is it nearer to God
Than the foot-hills, where the fountain
  Has carpeted earth with a sod?

'Tis not the fault of the poet—
  'Tis the reader demanding bosh ;
The world is silly—they know it,
  And they give it pumpkin for squash.
They know the world is æsthetic,
  Brought up in the æsthetic school,
And physic, or an emetic,
  Has the same effect on a fool.

MY DOUBTS.

If our God we cannot please
  By loving our poor neighbor,
Need we our Creator tease
  With our love and labor?
Shall God still forgive our sin,
  While we pinch our debtor?
Do these dollars we rake in
  Make our hard hearts better?

BACK AGAIN.

Seventy-five I am to-day,
My teeth are gone, my hair is gray ;
But it does seem the shortest dream
Since I set sail on life's rough stream.
I sailed in a circular course away,
With heart so light, dancing all day,
And now I trace the starting place—
In ev'ry nook I see a face
That long ago sailed out with me
On life's strange, mysterious sea.

I'm back again to childhood's port,
My thoughts are all of the old sort,
And mem'ry seems, with childhood dreams,
To harmonize the two extremes,
And only thoughts come back to me
I gathered at my mother's knee.
Again I feel I'd love to kneel
Down at her feet, and there appeal
For her dear loving hand again
To lead me through this world of pain.

Again my father's face I see—
Out through shadows it smiles on me ;
My brothers, too, come into view,
All smiling as they use to do ;
My sisters all smile up to me,

Just like the old times use to be,
And old dog Gale, with wagging tail,
I see him coming down the trail
Where the wild rabbits use to run,
And gave us boys tremendous fun.

'Tis three score and ten years—ah me !
Since I clung to my mother's knee.
The trip is o'er, I'm back on shore—
Back to the starting place once more.
And there's no mem'ry left to me,
No faces that I use to see,
Except the few around me grew
In childhood, now again in view :
Only this mem'ry is left to me
As I look over life's rough sea.

THE CONTRAST.

Little trousers, great big holes,
Corporations without souls,
Little wages, great big work,
Small men suffer, big men shirk,
Little feet with great big smell,
Little heaven, great big hell :
Thus in life I'm finding all
The real good things awful small.

WHILE BETSEY PLAYED THE ORGAN.

Betsey at the organ playing
   "Home, sweet HOME," that plaintive song ;
At my feet the old dog staying,
   Stops to listen, sighs ere long.
Does he hear my own heart sighing,
   While my thoughts go far away?
For he starts a dismal crying,
   Just as tho' his lips would say :

"Master, I know how you're thinking
   Of the home of former days,
And your heart is softly drinking
   These sad thoughts the organ plays :
To your mind it brings a shadow
   Of the old home 'mongst the trees,
And you seem to see the meadow,
   Hear the sighing Summer breeze."

Does he see that home neglected
   On the iris of my eye—
Picture of that home reflected,
   Which I see myself, and sigh ?
Does the music softly ringing
   Both our hearts in mem'ry lave?
Do familiar voices, singing,
   Seem to come back from the grave?

Does he see my pale lips quiver?
  Sad tears from my lashes start?
While dear Betsey, God forgive her,
  Plays "Sweet Home" upon my heart?
Cease your moaning, dog or devil,
  For you read my soul too well!
Beast of sympathy, or evil,
  Can you future scenes foretell?

Will I see this dear home ever
  Where my childhood mem'ries sleep?
Where around the door so clever
  Morning glories use to creep?
But the old dog ceases crying,
  Lays his head upon the floor,
Moans in answer to my sighing,
  Seems to say: "Oh, never more!"

Are your moans commiserate
  For the longings in my breast?
Will I ever leave this desert
  For the old home in the East?
And the organ still is crying
  While the old dog on the floor
Seems to answer to my sighing:
  "Never, never, never more!"

HAPPY! HAPPY NEW YEAR!

Happy new year, here you are!
You're not welcome, I declare.
If you know how sad I am,
You would know I'm playing sham.
When I say I welcome you
Back again, like folks all do.
What care you for such as I?
What care you how soon I die?
You are only moving on,
Doing work you cannot shun.
Ev'ry year you come around,
Walking on the frozen ground,
Calling me a weakly thing,
Caring not if in the spring
Pneumonia or consumptive cough
Comes and snatches me right off.

Happy new year! bah, such bosh!
Hand me down my Mackintosh ;
You are bringing rain or snow
Ev'ry time your face you show.
You are counting wrinkles, too,
On my face, were lines you drew ;
Stroking down my scanty hair,
To observe the silver there ;

Patting me on my bald place,
Saying I've run all to face;
Bearing on with bad intent,
Just to make my body bent :
Touch my teeth with foul decay,
Take my keen eye-sight away.
Happy new year! bah, such stuff!
How we liars play you bluff!

Happy new year! now that's rum
Since we hate to see you come :
Even maidens, old and tough,
Try to play on you this bluff;
Treat you in a style so soft,
But ashamed to tell how oft
You have pass'd them on the road,
Since in market they have stood
Waiting, as their friends all know;
Fishing, too, to catch a beau.
They'd a durn sight rather you
Never came back into view,
Unless it should be your plan
To fetch that long-looked-for man ;
And each year then, with the snow,
Bring some fresh heir, don't you know?

LOOKING DOWN THE ROAD.

There's a curious melancholy
    Seems to fall upon the mind,
When we remember friends so jolly
    Who are strewed along the line;
And it seems to be such folly
    Looking down the road behind;
Oh, such melancholy folly,
    Looking down the road behind.

When I look down this road behind me,
    Where the plant of mem'ry blooms,
Chains of sorrow come and bind me,
    And then lead me through Death's rooms;
Memory's tendrils then entwine me,
    As I walk among the tombs:
Oh, sad recollections find me,
    As I walk among the tombs.

And, all along this road, the living
    Are so swiftly turning gray,
And stern nature—unforgiving,
    Is carrying them away:
It is so melancholy living
    Among gloomy tombs all day—
Oh, such melancholy living,
    Looking at these graves alway.

Looking down this road at sunset,
    Through the opalescent light—
Far down life's narrow runlet,
    Until lost in mem'ry's night,
Where we boys had so much fun, yet
    So much labor in life's fight:
Oh, I seem to be the last one left,
    Walking in the tombs to-night.

Oh, I am sad to-night, don't mind me,
    And I seem no longer brave;
For each step down the road behind me
    Seems to be an old friend's grave;
And the shadows all remind me
    That the happiness I crave
Is not down the road behind me,
    Where each footstep strikes a grave.

The links of friendship time did sever
    Lay along this road behind,
And I see old faces clever
    Beaming on me, loving, kind:
Friends are gone from this life forever—
    I am weeping—never mind;
I will try my best endeavor
    To forget this road behind.

A CHILD OF FATE.

On the banks of the Bald Eagle,
 Many, many years ago,
There was born of humble parents,
 When the skies were filled with snow,
A little son, weak and fragile,
 With a slender hold on life;
But he lived and grew to manhood,
 Battled with a world of strife.

Years of struggles, years of danger,
 Midst them all he lived and grew;
Three times the Bald Eagle water
 Hid his bare-foot form from view.
But each time the boy was rescued,
 And brought back again to life;
Child of fate and circumstances,
 Born to hardships and to strife.

Far across the troubled ocean,
 Where the Danube waters flow,
There was born a German maiden,—
 Who she was you soon will know;
For her parents were ambitious,
 And a feeling of unrest
Filled their souls with a strange longing
 For a land far in the West.

And this little German maiden
　　Cross'd the mighty, trackless sea;
Left behind a narrow kingdom,
　　Found this broad land of the free.
Fate had, too, prepared a lover
　　For the little German maid,
And the boy from the Bald Eagle
　　In her presence one day strayed.

What strange law, and what strange reason
　　Caused her young heart to beat?
And the boy from the Bald Eagle
　　Lays his poor heart at her feet.
Why should these two meet as lovers?
　　Why should both hearts palpitate?
What strange law brought them together?
　　If it's not the hand of fate.

These two strange souls were united;
　　Fate ordained it should be so;
Sons were born, and, of that number,
　　There is one GRIT readers know.
If the boy from the Bald Eagle,
　　And the maid from Danube's shore,
Were not brought by fate together,
　　And each other to adore;

If the waters of Bald Eagle,
　　When they swallowed up the lad,
Had not been robbed of their victim,
　　Would the maid a lover had?

If they had not met as lovers,
   And five sturdy sons begat.
If they ne'er had seen each other,
   Where, oh, where would I be at!

MY CREED.

Loving man has been my creed,
   With pity for the lowly ;
Binding hearts where sorrows bleed,
   This working passage slowly
O'er the rugged stream of life,
   Where mortal man is sailing,
Ships are sinking in the strife,
   And hearts of Captains failing.
If I see my brother's ship
   Crippled beyond sailing,
I must help retain his grip,
   And lend a hand at bailing.

ART.

The dog with the sawed-off tail,
   And the dudelet, so awfully smart,
And the summer girl dressed like a male—
   They are all a poor work of art.

THOUGHTS ON THEOSOPHY.

Why do I dream of things—
Shadows of unknown wings—
Sleep to my mem'ry brings
    While in repose?
Whence come these thought-light beams,
Even in mid-day dreams?
Life a strange myst'ry seems—
    Only God knows.

Thoughts I ne'er heard before
Knock at my memory door.
Pass away, come no more
    To me again;
Then, on some other day,
Stranger thoughts come to stay,
Burdens upon me lay,
    Where joy has lain.

Has my soul, all unknown,
From an existence flown,
Where it has slowly grown,
    Beyond our ken?
Has this soul I hold dear—
Passing through trials here—
Lived on this mundane sphere
    In other men?

And, in the years to come,
Must this world be its home,
Go back into the womb,
        Be born again?
Must it this cold world trod,
And, ere it goes abroad,
Become as pure as God—
        Free from all stain?

If this soul is to live
With its God, I believe
We our poor souls deceive
        With death and pain:
For death is but a rest,
Soul freed from mortal breast:
When God knows it is best,
        We live again.

If God created all
Long ere poor Adam's fall,
All He needs is to call
        Souls from the air;
And, at a new child's birth,
Souls that belong to earth
Send a companion forth,
        Child-life to share.

So may it ever be,
Until each soul is free;
All of God's love to see,
        And be His own:

Life here is but a day,
Death but a night, they say;
Ages must pass away
    Ere we're full grown.

What do we know of life
Outside its pain and strife?
All sorts of faith is rife—
    Who knows the right?
Better far not to know,
Else God would tell us so,
And we must groping go
    Out in the night.

SOCIETY.

Proudly marching, dainty feet,
    Hands too soft for using ;
Blood wrung from poor hearts they eat—
    Ah, 'tis so amusing
Walking on the upturned face
    Of a starving neighbor,
Crushing hands at ev'ry pace,
    Crushing hearts with labor.
Lordly castles dripping blood,
    Where sighs, like zephyrs, blowing ;
Silks and satin steeped in flood
    Of widow's tears, while sewing.

LIFE.

Oh, Life, you are the strangest thing!
Poets of your mystery sing.
None know the place whence you have come,
Or why you left your far-off home.
In my own body you did creep
At some time while I lay asleep.
I do not know where we first met;
I try to think it out, but yet
I cannot think of any time,
Of such oblivion sublime,
When you and I were set apart,
And there was silence in my heart;
When these two eyes were closed and blind,
And no thought lived within my mind,
When I could neither feel nor think—
Without a thought or bare instinct—
When I was scattered in the air,
In the earth, and everywhere,—
Now where did you exist, ere we
Were joined in this strange mystery?

Oh, was it in the day or night
When first we met? and was it right
That you should dwell within my skin
Without permission to move in?

And when you forced my heart to move,
Was it selfishness or love?
And all these little aches and pains—
Of which a mem'ry still remains—
Within my little body frail,
When doctors tried, without avail,
To make you live more at your ease,
And not so much my body tease,—
Were you then of Death afraid?
And were calling loud for aid?
Were then each pain and ache your cry,
To warn me that, if you should die,
The air would me dissolve again,
And put me back where I had lain
Before you came in search of me,
And brought me out of mystery?

Oh, Life, tell me, are we true friends?
Since nature sometime soon intends
To part us, and drive you away,
And turn my body to decay,
Why don't you let me speak to you?
Why don't we meet in friendship true?
Why don't you tell me all you know,
And what you think of things below?
Why can't you tell me, out of love,
If there is a great world above?
Where you will go when you depart,
And leave but silence in my heart.
Are you immortal—do you know?

Oh, tell me all this ere you go.
Tell me, tell me, oh, tell me true!
What relation am I to you?
And why this silence, oh, my friend?
Or do you cruelly intend
To go off some sad, dreary day,
And leave my body to decay?

Ah, Life, are you but part of me?
Is it with my dim eyes you see?
Is it with my weak heart you feel,
And in like mortal weakness kneel
Down at the feet of myst'ry deep—
Where all the tongues of knowledge sleep,
And will not answer those who ask
The gods of mystery to unmask:
And show us mortals all we crave
To know of things beyond the grave?
Ah, Life, you may be asking me
Concerning these strange things we see:
You may imagine that 'tis I
God has intended shall not die;
And you may wonder where I go,
When I have disappeared below.
Oh, if we had a language known
To both of us, how very soon
At loggerheads we both would be,
Discussing immortality.

LIFE'S BLOODY BATTLE.

Oh, life is only a battle,
　With poverty and disease;
I hear all around the rattle
　Of the falling yellow leaves:
Yellow leaves that fought all summer
　Against the hail and the frost;
They fall now without a murmur;
　They fought to the death—and lost.

The storms beat down on the mountains,
　The ocean lashes the shore,
The streams charge down from the fountains
　Like gladiators at war:
There's no time for words or praying,
　There is no time for remorse:
Hold fast where the great rocks are laying,
　And only be moved by force.

The birds and the beasts are fighting,
　The big fish eat the small;
But, true as I am writing,
　There's only defeat for all.
In life's fight there is no quarter,
　So brace your back to the wall;
Your blood will mix with the mortar,
　And stain the earth where you fall.

Are you weary fighting, brother?
  Do you wish the battle o'er?
Would you swop this world for another,
  Where mortals never explore?
Ah, you dare not shirk this battle,
  Or refuse a warrior's grave ;
You must fear not death's harsh rattle,
  For the world loves only the brave.

A BAD COUGH.

There's the whooping cough,
  And consumption cough,
But the very worst cough, I declare,
  Is to take your mash,
  And cough up your cash
For the heathen, at a church fair.
  There's the whisky cough,
  And dyspeptic cough,
But the cough that will Christians surprise,
  Is to never shirk,
  But cough up good work
Until you land in Paradise.

MYSELF.

I wonder if some writer, in future years,
    Will write a biography of me.
And will he know of my struggles, and my tears,
    And how ambitious I use to be?
No; no one will know the secrets of my soul,
    No one will know my longings and strife,
No one will know how I tried to reach the goal,
    No one will know my most secret life.

Will he call me by the name I long have known,
    And say to the world: "He was a man
Who never had inspirations of his own—
    His soul was of the prosaic plan?"
And will the world then think it knows my story,
    After reading those few careless lines?
Believing that I simply wrote for glory?
    And not for paltry dollars and dimes?

Are they only noble who write for glory—
    Who have large fortunes already won,
Whose ancestors have always lived in story—
    Who ask praise only for all they've done?
And shall I, because I have written for bread,
    Be despised for my lowly labor?
Spoken of in pity after I am dead,
    By my aristocratic neighbor?

They will never know my history—never!
    There is a world within me unknown,
Even to myself, and this world forever
    Shall be a desert when life has flown.
For even I am yet a total stranger
    Within these strange walls of flesh and bone ;
Trembling so often at some unknown danger,
    And fearing to meet grim Death alone.

No ! nobody will ever tell my secrets,
    For no one can read my secret mind ;
They will know not my longings, sorrows, regrets,
    And these are the life of all mankind.
Even could my own eyes look back and see,
    From that strange dreamland beyond the tomb,
Ah, they might drop a pitying tear for me,
    Knowing how blindly I met my doom.

Even my dearest friends, who daily see me,
    Know not the strange secrets of my mind :
And do you think, when death at last shall free me,
    All my secrets will be left behind ?
No ; when I leave this world of pain and sorrow,
    My longings shall melt into the air,
And the whole world, after death's to-morrow,
    Will forget that I was ever here.

PHILOSOPHY OF THE HAT.

The man who wears his hat on the back of his head,
    With his hair pasted down on his forehead,
You can make up your mind that his pride is not dead,
    Tho' his looks may be utterly horrid.

If he wears his beaver down over his ear,
    And then tilted his one eye quite over,
He feels good enough to have thousands a year,
    And is up to his crupper in clover.

If he tilts the brim downward square over his eyes,
    And cocked up behind like a feather,
Oh, you'll find him a trickster then, to your surprise;
    And you'll not be long trav'ling together.

If he wears his new hat square on top of his head,
    And it looks as tho' it was too small,
You may make up your mind that he's genteelly bred,
    But no good to the big world at all.

If he wears his hat firmly, and squarely, and straight,
    Neither cocked up in front nor behind,
He may carry a brain that is moving the state,
    With a heart that is loving and kind.

But, if it seems crowded far down on his ears,
   And they look so lopped-over and flabby,
He's either a skinflint, grown harder with years,
   Or, he may be half-witted and shabby.

So be careful, young man, how you're wearing your hat,
   For your character shines out from under;
And the people who see you will put you down pat,
   For a man, or a nuisance, by thunder.

MY FARM.

When a boy I use to labor
   Ev'ry summer on the farm,
For my richest, nearest neighbor,
   Doing work of ev'ry form.
In the hot sun, weak and weary,
   How I often longed for shade!
How I envied farmer Cleary,
   And positions longed to trade.

How I wished to be the owner
   Of a farm with such broad fields,
For I thought I'd ten times sooner
   Live on what the rich soil yields,
Than to work for such small money
   Fourteen hours ev'ry day,
Like the poor bee storing honey
   For some one to take away.

One day my old father, guessing
  What was passing in my mind,
Said, "There is no use thus distressing
  Your head with thoughts of this kind;
For you own a territory
  Richer than these fields are here,
Where you can win cash and glory,
  If you go to plowing there.

You've a casket filled with treasure
  That will each year profit yield;
In the shade, and at your pleasure,
  You can cultivate this field.
And it needs no fertilizer,
  If you cultivate with care,
And ev'ry year be growing wiser,
  If you do your plowing there."

Since that day I have been toiling
  In the field of which he spoke,
But at first it seemed hard moiling—
  Aching heart at every stroke.
Bitter weeds in corners growing—
  Weeds of envy and disdain;
These I pulled up, so well knowing
  They would smother golden grain.

Now that field is paying profit
  More than Cleary's whole estate,
And its fruit—a sample of it
  Is in this tale I relate.

'T was my think-pot I've been plowing,
Raising nonsense for the press.
"Small potatoes," you're avowing—
Well, they'll pay to dig, I guess.

———

DESERT HEART.

———

Out on the desert the scorching heat
Down on the barren gray sand does beat,
So hot that it burns the trav'ler's feet,
    And the earth is crying for rain:
Far in the distance the whirl-winds dance,
Over the sand hills they gaily prance,
While the great silence our souls entrance,
    And our heart sings this sad refrain:

Where are the flowers which bloom in spring,
And to the desert their fragrance bring?
Here is the dry stem, poor withered thing,
    Left bleaching since touched by Death.
Ah, where are the joys, of my soul a part,
Joys of life's spring time, before the smart
Of sorrows left their stems in my heart;
    How they rattle in mem'ry's breath!

Now life is but withered stems to me,
Death is the desert Eternity;
After I cross it what will there be?
    Is there water beyond the range?
Plodding along in the desert sand,
Passively holding to Hope's frail hand,
Shall we cross over to some fair land?
    Ah, neighbor, this journey seems strange.

Hand-boards erected along the way
Speak of a country where endless day
Reigns forever, and there, too, they say,
    Sweet flowers forever will bloom.
This land, they say, is beyond our ken,
Never beheld by the eyes of men;
'T is only a dream land—ah, then,
    It leaves us so much to presume.

Alone I 'm walking the desert sand,
Even unclasped from hope's frail hand,
Going blindly to that unknown land,
    Simply going because I must.
With all the pain from sun's heat severe,
While all the flowers begin to sear,
I would rather stay forever here,
    Than go back to the desert dust.

MY LOVE STORY.

Oh, was n't it strange to you and me,
When we sat in the parlor long ago;
    Both hearts as loving as love could be,
    And we said that through all eternity
    I belonged to you, and you to me,
And your eyes were bright with love's sweet glow.

We knew of a parting soon to come
That would take you thousands of miles away,
    And we thought of it like creatures dumb;
    It seemed so hard to be parted from
    The one we loved, and the dear old home
Seemed full of sadness that autumn day.

Oh, how we lingered that autumn day,
And my hand, unthinking, your hand sought;
    Your drooping head on my shoulder lay,
    And we thought of you going far away,
    And the only words of hope we could say :
Our love is too pure to come to naught.

I slipped a ring on your passive hand,
And kissed the lips upturned to mine,
    And thought to myself, oh, love is grand !
    No sweeter blessing could gods demand;
    So tender, yet such a mighty band,
Stronger than chains our hearts entwine.

For two long years, yes, almost three,
After you wandered from that spot,
   Only in mem'ry I lived with thee,
   And in my dreams your face could see;
   But these old, old words came back to me :
Our love is too pure to come to naught.

How strange it seems to me and mine
To meet again far from that spot ;
   To feel our loving arms entwine,
   To kiss those lips upturned to mine,
   To see those eyes so loving shine,
With a love too pure to come to naught.

POOR FARMER BOY.

What makes the sky so blue,
   Oh, farmer boy ?
Why sing the birds for you,
   Poor, farmer boy ?
Why are the fields so green ?
Fairer than ever seen ;
There is a cause, I ween,
   Oh, farmer boy.

All your clothes are so coarse,
   Oh, farmer boy ;
And shoes even worse,
   Poor farmer boy ;

Coarse is the food you eat,
Tho' it may taste so sweet,
Back in your lone retreat.
  Poor farmer boy.

Go whistling to your plow,
  Oh, farmer boy ;
I know your secret now,
  Poor farmer boy :
All you love are near to you,
Friends, and all dear to you;
There comes no fear to you,
  Oh, farmer boy.

Over the fields, I know,
  Oh, farmer boy,
Tripping gaily to and fro,
  Poor farmer boy ;
There is a maiden fair,
With country beauty rare—
Your heart is always there,
  Poor farmer boy.

What care you for the strife,
  Oh, farmer boy ;
Or for another life,
  Poor farmer boy :
Home is the world to you,
Where all the friends are true,
Sweet'ning your work for you,
  Oh, farmer boy.

Build castles in the air,
  Oh, farmer boy,
And put your sweetheart there,
  Poor farmer boy;
Long not for other joys,
Like the proud city boys,
Who fill their life with toys,
  Poor farmer boy.

Here is where great men grow,
  Oh, farmer boy,
Some time you, too, may go,
  Poor farmer boy;
Far above the city man,
Who lives to scheme and plan,
But seldom leads the van,
  Poor farmer boy.

Go whistling to your plow,
  Oh, farmer boy;
I know your secret now,
  Poor farmer boy:
You love the sky so blue,
And all the green fields, too,
And some one who loves you,
  Oh, farmer boy.

WHEN DADDY SAID THE BLESSING.

I am sitting by the window
    In my far-off western home,
But my mind goes off a dreaming,
    And refuses back to come;
For I love to dwell on events
    That occurred so long ago,
When we were all boys together,
    And were bent on mischief so:
The faces we made at table,
    When our mother felt so shocked,
While our daddy said the blessing
    With his eyes half cocked.

We boys were never so pious
    That we could sit still, and wait
Until the blessing was finished,
    With our eyes upon the plate;
But we'd pinch each other slyly,
    Or pull at the old dog's tail,
And make faces at the baby,
    Who would then set up a wail;
But at times we felt dad's knuckles
    Just where our bangs were docked,
For he sometimes said the blessing
    With his eyes half cocked.

But mother seemed to love us, so
    She kept our secrets well,
And all our deeds must be quite mean
    To make her up and tell;
And we had lots of fun always
    When our daddy's eyes were shut,
And when his dear old back was turned
    We dropped in the noisy rut;
And, even at the table, we
    All decent manners shocked,
While our daddy said the blessing
    With his eyes half cocked.

Oh, that dear old, kind old daddy!
    And that sweet old mother dear!
How often I have wished of late
    I could have them with me here;
But life is, oh, so very short!
    And our joys so weak and frail,
That even when we laugh too loud,
    We wind up with a wail;
And old grim Fate seems to watch us
    With his hands before him locked,
Like when daddy said the blessings
    With his eyes half cocked.

DREAMLAND FACES.

"Sweet dreamland faces, dancing to and fro,
Bring back to mem'ry days of long ago."
So sang the stranger, gazing in the stream,
Seeing lov'd faces pictured in his dream:
Down where the waters turn to deepest blue,
Where cluster faces who once lov'd him true.
But these dear faces quickly disappear,
For on the water drops a bitter tear.

Sweet dreamland faces, come to me again!
Tho' you give heart-ache and such homesick pain,
No more my teardrops shall obscure its view
While looking tenderly on faces true.
Down in the bosom of the flowing stream,
Come back the faces of mem'ry's dream—
Home of my childhood pictured in the deep,
Even the bed-room where I used to sleep.

There stands my father with his aged form,
His long hair frosted in life's chilly storm;
And my old mother standing by his side,
Seems to look on me with the same old pride.
See her smile gently, while her tender eyes
Light up so loving with glad surprise.
Dear God in heaven, Father of the stream!
Will the resurrection be like this dream?

There stand my brothers looking in my face,
Each line familiar, easily to trace!
Some of them living, some of them asleep,
But all seem wakened, pictured in the deep:
They all seem life-like in their worldly homes,
For here in dreamland grim death never comes.
But my heart is aching with silent pain,
Dear God in heaven! shall we meet again?

Sweet dreamland faces, speak, oh, speak to me!
Will you all meet me in eternity?
Are thoughts of heaven only like a dream—
Only a picture shadowed on life's stream!
Will death make ripples, blotting out the view—
Hiding forever these pictures of you?
Dear God in heaven, let, oh let me know,
When ends this dreamland, whither shall I go?

LOVE.

Ah, there is but one love true—
    Love so deep that it is blind,
Giving the whole world up for you
    And leaving home and friends behind.

THE BULLY.

The man who wants to slap your face
    For disputing things not true,
Would shoot you down within your place,
    If caught burglarizing you.

THE CRIES GO UP TO HEAVEN.

Last night I dreamed that I sat up in heaven,
  And very close to the celestial throne,
Where I could hear, every day of the seven,
  The prayer of the world and its bitter moan,
  Crying for mercy in beseeching tone.

"Lord, thou hast forsaken us!" cried the starving;
  "Our strong brothers rob us of all we get;
We do all the digging, delving and carving,
  Exposed to the snow, the frost and the wet,
  And still we have never seen justice yet.

"O, Lord, I am weary! Lord, I am dying!
  Oh, so hungry and cold! and do you care?
Have you turned a deaf ear unto our crying,
  And forsaken the poor everywhere—
  Paying no heed to their bitter prayer?

"Lord, did you make us in days of creation
  To be poor slaves—to be never satisfied,
To bear the heavy burdens of this nation,
  While the proud aristocrats us deride?
  Did you intend Justice in wealth's divide?"

And I dreamed I looked on the struggling masses,
  As they writhed and twisted in their greed for gold;
And I saw the pride of the haughty classes,
  While the hungry masses were bought and sold,
  And the orphan suffered hunger and cold.

And I noticed that, one day out of seven,
 They went to their churches to offer up prayer;
Expecting that words would take them to heaven,
 From the hell of man's own creation here—
 From the hunger and pain felt ev'rywhere.

And the angels whispered to one another:
 "How the poor suffer under greed's rod!
For the rich won't own the poor man his brother.
 How hardly shall they see the Kingdom of God!
 As Jesus had said when this earth he trod."

READY TO GO.

I useter look on death an' dyin'
 As a dretful, orful thing,
An' I couldn't keep from cryin',
 An' my hands I useter wring,
When grim Death 'u'd come an' carry
 Dear old frien's right from my side,
An' I'd feel so orful sorry
 While behint the hearse I'd ride.

But so many hev gone over
 To that place they talk about
In the meetin', an' where clover
 Grows knee-high, an' there, no doubt,

They are happy doin' nuthin'
But a playin' harps ov gold,
An' their angel stomachs stuffin'
Jist as full as they kin hold.

An' this world is not so jolly
As it was when I was young,
An' at times a melancholy
Over my poor heart is sprung;
An' at ev'nin', settin' smokin',
Thinkin' ov these frien's so true,
Sumthin' in my breast comes chokin',
An' I wanter be dead, too.

Even if death is but sleepin'—
That beats this world, at its best,
For there'd be no hunger creepin'—
Jist a lazyin' at rest.
While I'm settin' smokin', weary,
Lis'nin' to the wind's soft ''woo-oo !''
This here world seems growin' dreary,
An' I wanter be dead, too.

If these frien's that has gone over
To this world ov joy an' peace,
Are a wallowin' in clover
Where the noon-spells never cease;
An' such sights as they are seein' !
An' there's nuthin' else ter do
But jist everlastin' bein'
Jolly, an' a singin', too.

What's the use ov me a missin'
All the good times over there?
Where the summer winds is kissin'
An' a blowin' through your hair.
All my best frien's hev departed,
An' there's nuthin' else ter do
But ter die, an' then be carted
Over to the boneyard, too.

HE SHOCKED THE WORLD.

Onc't there was a little boy who wanted to be seen ;
He was very tall and slender, and freckle-faced, and lean.
He longed to become famous, and win praise and renown,
And be the one admired boy of all the boys in town.
He longed to be a hero, and have people at his feet,
To select the best of all things, and give him just the sweet.
When he was told to do the chores, he'd only laugh and
    mock,
And give his folks and relatives the meanest kind of shock.
But he had great ambitions to become, oh, very rich,
To be president, or gov'nor, he didn't care just which ;
But he wanted things to come to him of their own accord,
And all he'd hafter do would be to just set down and board.
He only wish't to set all day in the shade and dream,
And have the good things come to him, like bubbles on a
    stream ;

But if you'd speak of study, he'd only laugh and mock,
And say, if he could not win fame, he'd give the world a
   shock.
Long before he was a man, all his people knew
There was no kind of honest work this boy would do;
So they prayed for him in meetin', when he was there,
But he'd set and make faces durin' the hull pray'r.
But he thought, somehow, that fortune was bound to come,
Just because he wish't it, and knew more than some
People gave him credit for, and some day, by jocks,
He'd give the world and neighbors some gee-menshly
   shocks.
I know lots of boys like him, dear reader, don't you?
So in love with themselves that there's nothin' they
   will do;
But will set and build castles all the day long,
And picture themselves like the man in the song;
The owner of horses, fine houses and land,
And just lay on the divan, and never turn their hand
To do toilin', or spinnin', or darnin' of socks,
But just have successes that'll give the world shocks.
Well, this boy that I mentioned, he grew to manhood,
And never was known to do one stroke of good;
But kept longin' for glory, for fame and renown,
And to be the biggest mogul in the hull town;
So he soon took to stealin', then robbin' a store—
Was 'rested for murder, and for sheddin' of gore.
And, even on the gallows, he set there and mocked;
But his neck was soon broken—the world it was shocked.

LIFE IS ALL GUESS-WORK.

This life is a thing uncertain,
　　Begins and ends like a dream;
It starts from behind a curtain,
　　Then flows to an unknown stream.
The future is merely guessing,
　　The past a struggle severe;
We call ev'rything a blessing
　　That keeps us existing here.

In childhood we dream of conquest,
　　Of things we'll do when full grown;
Our friends will be ev'ryone blest
　　With riches that's all our own.
We'll marry the fairest creature,
　　Who will own half of this sphere;
Her other redeeming feature
　　Will be, calling us her "dear."

We make ourself a liar,
　　A boaster, and thing so vain;
In secret we do aspire
　　To see all our rivals slain,
We picture ourself in battle,
　　With blood dripping from our sword—
Voice sounding above the rattle,
　　Defiance in ev'ry word.

But soon all these castles vanish—
    We wed a maid with cold feet;
All sleep from our eyes she'll banish,
    And make our mis'ry complete.
She'll double up on the pillow
    Like an Irish peddler's pack,
And, worse than a North sea billow,
    Are her cold feet to our back.

And then will the rent collector,
    And the money-lending shark,
And the social-line inspector
    Be making this old world dark.
Our future is now uncertain,
    We know not the date or day,
When Death will hoist the curtain,
    And move us out of the way.

It's all sheer nonesense for preachers
    Marking out a path in life,
For even the best of teachers
    Are meeting with unseen strife:
It is all groping and guessing,
    From the hour we are born,
And we only get the blessing
    Like the blind pig got the corn.

LITTLE NELL.

Of my early childhood dreaming,
  Sitting on the vine-clad stoop,
Where the moonlight comes in streaming,
  And the climbing roses droop;
    Sitting musing,
    Scenes confusing
  Come back, mem'ry disabusing;
And dear childhood faces beaming
  Through the shadows on the stoop,
Where the climbing roses, seeming
  Like the heads of children, droop.

Away back in the shadows misty
  Hanging o'er the days of yore,
I see myself and Nellie Listlie
  Sliding down the cellar door.
    Ma's prediction
    Of the friction,
  Beyond doubt or contradiction—
Said she, as she stooped and kissed me:
  "You must not slide any more;
For no cloth can ever resist the
  Friction of the cellar door."

But we kept on gently sliding,
  For such joys the soul enchants.
Says I, "Nell," as we went gliding,
  "*You* can't strike matches on *your* pants!"

Says she, grinning,
Sweetly winning,
"I tould do it at bedinnin',
But dis slidin', an' dis glidin'
Wif you on dis door each day,
(Dere's no use de setret hidin'),
I haint no more built dat way."

Drooping head and sweetly blushing
As we climbed the door so steep,
And we heard my mother hushing
Little brother back to sleep;
Says Nell, turning,
With face burning,
And with one hand me she's spurning:
"Do away, an' don't you tease me,
Tause you don't know what I see.
Did you spile your pants ter please me?
You're edzactly built like me!"

Little Nellie! long years sleeping
In the church-yard over there;
And the years so surely creeping,
Scatter silver in my hair.
Soon I'll meet her,
And will greet her,
In a world more fair and sweeter,
And I hope to find her sliding
Down the door eternity;
Whisp'ring to the Lord, confiding:
"He's edzactly built like me."

IONE.

There's a lone grave far out on the silent prairie,
  Where only the sighing winds and the coyote's howl is
    heard.
Here sleeps Ione, once as beautiful as a fairy,
  And whose song was once sweeter than the song of a
    bird.

The great sand storms in the summer sometimes sweep
    over
  The deep-sunken grave where the Indian maiden sleeps,
And the snow in winter falls deep enough to cover
  The devil-tongue cactus, where the primrose creeps.

There's a silence in the air that makes one feel dreary,
  Broken only now and then by the crow overhead;
And while you stand alone, your mind debates the query,
  If such solitude is not even felt by the dead.

Ione was but a dark-eyed, dusky half-breed maiden,
  Her father a white trader, and her mother a Ute.
She fell in love with a hunter, dashing Dick Hayden,
  Who returned her true affections, and soon won his suit.

But there was an Indian lover for the maiden,
  The wily hunter and trailer, the big, brave Ahmeek;
And he had sworn to kill the bold hunter, Dick Hayden,
  And for a chance to slay him the Indian did seek.

So, Ione and her lover, at the midnight hour,
  Stole silently away from her grandfather's tepee;
And each took a horse, saying it was Ione's dower,.
  And rode away in the darkness, with hearts light and
    free.

Over mountains, down canons they rode, silence keeping;
  Down deep gulches, across arroyos, onward they ride,
While the old grandfather in his tepee is sleeping,
  Never dreaming that the hunter has stolen his bride.

But the Indian, Ahmeek, soon discovers
  That the maiden he loved with the white hunter has fled;
He is soon mounted and in pursuit of the lovers,
  And each leap of the horse nods the gay plumes on his
    head.

Away on the lonely prairie, two days after,
  He overtakes the truants, and his keen blade leaps out;
Goaded on to madness by hearing their gay laughter,
  He holds aloft his knife and gives an exultant shout.

They meet, the rivals and the maiden; no word is spoken;
  But the lovers spur their horses and at each other dart;
The maiden rides between them, and both blows are broken,
  With the blades, aimed at each other, buried in her heart.

They pause, and, with great horror, they glance at each
    other.
"The great spirit has decided," the Indian said.
"We will bury our love in sorrow, now, my brother,
  And with our own wicked hands dig a grave for our
    dead."

Two days they sat there fasting; they are foes no longer;
    Now they both love the maiden in the spirit land;
They must be good friends now, for their hatred would
    wrong her;
And over Ione's grave they grasp each other's hand.

Then they both ride away, across the dreary prairie,
    The hunter to the east, the Indian to the west,
And left Ione sleeping—Ione, the dusky fairy—
    Ione, the half-breed maiden, now forever at rest.

RURAL MELODIES.

There is music in the meadows,
    There is music in the brush,
But exceptin' when it thunders,
    When there seems to be a hush.
Yes, but in the morning early
    When the sun begins to rise,
There's a thousand trills of music
    Goes ascending to the skies:
When the pigs cry for their breakfast
    In their little round log pen,
There's the "Kuck, kuck, kuck, chee-kaw-kuck!"
    Of the early layin' hen.

There's the robin on the pear tree
    Singin' "Purt, purt, purt, purt, purt!"
And the guinea in the meadow
    Yellin' jist as tho' 'twas hurt;
And the pee-wee on the stable
    Calls his wife, "My dear Phœbe,"
And the chick-a-dee is there, too,
    Singin' "Chick-a-dee, dee dee!"
And the swallows skim the heavens,
    And don't seem to care a darn
For the "Kuck, kuck, kuck, chee-káw-kuck!"
    Of the rooster in the barn.

And the farmer boy goes whistlin'
    On his way to start the plow,
And there's no fog horn to equal
    The loud bellow of the cow;
And the old black crow and raven
    That go soarin' over head
Send us down a caw so dismal,
    While they look for somethin' dead;
And there's the brown thrush, and jay bird,
    And the little jennie wren,
And the "Kuck, kuck, kuck, chee-kaw-kuck!"
    Of the cross old hatchin' hen.

Oh, there's music in the country,
    When the city's got the blues,
And the fields all over flowers
    In a thousand brilliant hues;
And the happy songs of nature
    Can be heard on ev'ry hill,

Minglin' with the gurglin' music
  Of the little ripplin' rill;
And the housewife saves the onions
  With some cuss words and with sticks,
Midst the "Kuck, kuck, kuck, chee-kaw-kuck!"
  Of the old hen with her chicks.

EBB AND FLOW.

Ebb and flow, come and go.
Just like the tide is our life below :
High-tide comes in, child life begins,
Roll on the shore in a frolicsome din.
Flow back tide, the old man died,
Swept to the ocean so deep and wide :
Come once more, leave a child at our door,
Take a grandfather with you when you leave the shore.
The waves come in, and the waves go back,
And the new come in on the old wave's track ;
Come and go, ebb and flow,
Youth comes in and age must go.
High on the wave child life does flow,
While age goes out in the under-tow.

Ships sail o'er midst the ocean's roar,
Just like our hopes sail evermore.
Hopes of to-day sail down the bay,
Out on the ocean and fade away ;

Toss'd on the deep where cruel rocks sleep,
Dashed to pieces—there's no time to weep.
Hopes good and stout, like ships, go out
Freighted with pleasure, sailing about ;
Some survive and come back again,
Some are lost on the raging main.
Some are wrecked within sight of land,
Like hopes that perish within our hand :
Come and go, ebb and flow,
We all go out in the under-tow.

Birds fly high in the summer sky,
Like our ambition when first we try ;
But, in the storm, they take alarm,
And fly to the shore to escape from harm ;
But next day, when storms clear away,
Birds and ambition fly over the bay :
Off and away in youth's fair day,
Never once resting—no delay :
On land and in sky, below and on high,
Sailing forever until we die :
Come and go, ebb and flow,
Back and forth we ever go :
What is beyond we do not know,
But we all go out in the under-tow.

AFTER MANY YEARS.

After years of journey,
    After many years,
I am back at home again
    Shedding glad, glad tears;
Friends are here to meet me,
Neighbors here to greet me,
Yet these seem sad, sad dreams,
    After many years.

When I went away, some friends
    Were just in their prime,
Now they are old and wrinkled,
    Showing tracks of time;
And here I meet again,
Down in the shady lane,
Some dear one I lov'd when young—
    Ah, is love a crime?

Shame-faced we meet again
    And hold out our hands;
Often I had thought of her
    While in other lands;
Holding her hand so tight,
    On this calm summer night,
Standing so meek—neither can speak,
    Make no demands.

. She is another's wife,
 And never again
Will she be my own sweetheart,
 Why do I remain?
One look into her eyes,
Find only there surprise—
So we part.   At my heart
 A queer, sad pain.

Passing on down the lane
 One last look I take,
Some impulse had caused her, too,
 The same move to make;
Tho' I am married, too,
And love my wife so true,
In some way all that day
 My heart did ache.

FROST BITES.

Oh, the leaves are turning yellow
 And are looking pale and sere,
And remind one of the gray hairs
 On the head of the old year ;
They are trembling in the breezes,
 And so hopelessly they fall
To old mother earth's cold bosom—
 The last resting place for all.

One by one the leaves are dropping,
  Like the mother's silent tears
On the grave of some beloved
  Of the long-past, happy years;
They are falling, falling, falling,
  Soon the trees will all be bare,
And their arms, so long and naked,
  Stand like beggars ev'rywhere.

I have seen the western farmer
  Stripped as bare, or even worse,
By the frosty money-lender
  And his cruel mortgage curse;
I have seen bare limbs of children
  In poverty's exposure,
When the homestead was frost-bitten
  By the mortgage's foreclosure.

And the farmer's hard-earned dollars,
  Like the sered and yellow leaf,
Keep on dropping, dropping, dropping,
  On the legal mortgage thief.
There's no hope for the poor farmer;
  There are no warm winds to bring
Back a bran-new suit of clothing,
  Like the trees get in the spring.

Oh, Jehovah's frosts are cruel,
  And no mercy do they show;
They delight to kill and slaughter,
  Spreading death where e'er they go;

But the yellow leaves now falling
Are not victims of a curse,
Like the blood-stained, hard-earned dollars
Squeezed from out the farmer's purse.

QUOTIN' SKRIPTOOR.

"Blessed are the poor in spirit"—read the preacher from
the book,
And the poor old mortgaged farmer raised up with a startled
look.

"That means you and me, Samantha; fur our speerits's
mighty low:
Since we signed that dad-bin mortgage we hain't got half
a show."

"For theirs is the kingdom of heav'n"—read the preacher
then again.

"That's all right fur us, Samantha, that's the promise,
plump and plain;
But our children, dog-gone-nation! what do they get in
the deal?
If there's not some explanation, don't you think they otter
squeal?

"The hairs of your head are numbered "—read the preacher
  then aloud,
And again the mortgaged farmer's face appeared above the
  crowd:

"Silas Cruncher, don't yo' hear him—hear what the good
  book has said?
A'most anny one could count them scatterin' hairs upon
  yo'r head.
But what I'd like ter know partic'lar, when old Cruncher's
  debt falls due,
When he goes up with low speerits, will St. Peter pass him
  through?
If he then presents the number of the hairs to heaven
  due,
And demands a full collection, what will we poor bald
  heads do?

"By its fruit the tree is known"—read the preacher louder
  still,

But the mortgaged farmer said, "You have gotter wait
  until
The fruit is ripe and full matoord, and jist reddy fur to
  fall,
Before you judge it right and square, and give justice
  plump ter all.
But that early apple tree in the corner of my lot,
I've been thinkin' all along is the best tree I have got;
But the duced gaul-darn boys, long before the fruit is ripe,
Come at night when I'm in bed and ev'ry dad-bim apple
  swipe.

" The wind bloweth where it listeth "—read the preacher
    louder yet,
And up jumped the mortgaged farmer: " That's the gospel
    truth, you bet!
Sometimes it blows through my whiskers in the gayest,
    wildest glee!
And right through my week-day trousers where the patches
    otter be.
Wind has got more dad-bim freedom than the people ever
    wish,
For it blows through Jones' barn yard, then right inter my
    soup dish."

Then the preacher closed the Bible,—he was mad for a
    divine,—
Quoting once more in conclusion, " Cast not pearls before
    the swine !"

THE CHIEF END OF MAN.

There's only one life to endure of,
    And only one death that we're sure of,
But we try to obtain the whole earth for gain,
    And shove God's miserable poor off.

THE SILENT SOMEWHERE.

See the man pose as a villain,
  So drunken, brutal, coarse and mean ;
He has murdered a civilian,
  Stained with blood the grass so green.
See him wave his knife so gory,
  While the moon shines bright above him :
Ah, if we only knew his story,
  Somewhere, sometime, some one loved him.

He was once a smiling baby,
  Pressed against a mother's breast,
And that mother somewhere, maybe,
  In her heart loves him still best.
See, he now beholds his victim ;
  No thought of remorse can move him,
Will that mother's heart convict him ?
  Somewhere, sometime then un-love him ?

And that woman, low and fallen,
  Reeling drunken through the street,
Somewhere some poor heart is calling
  God to stop her wandering feet.
Whisky will her conscience smother,
  Drown the thoughts that come to move her,
But she knows there is a mother
  Somewhere who will always love her.

Even in her sin and folly,
  When her thoughts go back to home,
In her sober melancholy,
  She knows that she still may come
Back to home, and back to mother,
  With the dear old roof above her.
Oh, this thought she cannot smother,
  Somehow she will always love her.

After this frail life has hurried
  Past us, like a fleeting breath,
And we all are dead and buried
  In the silent sleep of death,
Will these mothers in the somewhere,
  Un-like earthly mothers prove?
Will they, somehow, sometime find there
  They have lost their mother-love?

Oh, this something, sometime, somehow,
  Something we are hoping for !
Sometime something cannot come now
  On this side death's open door.
Somehow we hope to be found there
  In this somewhere up above ;
Somehow joys will then abound there,
  Tho' in hell are some we love.

SHE NEVER KNEW.

When I close my eyes in dreaming
 Of the dreary long ago,
There 's a little face comes beaming,
 Fills my heart with warmest glow;
For I knew her when a maiden,
 Saw her growing day by day,
When her soul with joy was laden,
 And she stole my heart away.

In my dreams and castles airy,
 And all hopes I held in view,
She was my sweet little fairy,
 But she never, never knew.

Long I used to sit and wonder
 How to win her little heart,
Dream all night, and all day ponder,
 Until love became a smart:
But she seemed so far above me,
 Fading daily from my view;
Still I prayed that she might love me,
 But she never, never knew.

When I thought she'd gone forever,
 Loved some one of wealth and fame,
Still 'twas useless to endeavor
 To forget her face and name.

Then I wrote her my sad letter,
  Told her how I loved her true,
But would go off and forget her,
  Since I'd told her all she knew.

Years have passed, and still I'm roaming,
  But to-day a letter came,
Asking when to her I'm coming,
  And was signed by her dear name.
She had lately found my letter,
  It was lost all these years through:
I was trying to forget her,
  And she never, never knew.

And she told me in her letter
  How her hair was turning gray,
But there is no bar or fetter
  That would drive my love away.
And she told me how she ever
  Loved me with a love so true,
And we should not grieve forever
  Over what she never knew.

Oh, the hearts that now are aching,
  Roaming far by land and sea,
Leaving other fond hearts breaking,
  All because they could not see.
And when old age comes on creeping,
  They may meet, these lovers true,
And they 'll cry, midst all their weeping:
  Oh, I never, never knew !

CHANGES.

The flowers are blooming as sweetly
  As they did in the long ago,
And the birds are feathered as neatly,
  The cock has the same boastful crow;
But the songs of the birds seem older,
  And more commonplace to me;
The winds of the winter seem colder—
  Nothing seems like it used to be.

When the world was stranger and newer,
  And I was then only a boy,
When sorrows were lighter and fewer,
  And ev'rything filled me with joy,
The days seemed much longer and merry,
  And all nature seemed filled with glee;
Now the world seems changed in a flurry,
  But the changes are all in me.

The boys who are now in the meadows,
  Who are playing the games of old,
There's none of them heeding the shadows,
  There's none of them heeding the cold;
And they 're just as happy as we were,
  And the days are as long and free,
And I'd give all the world to be there,
  Without all these changes in me.

Life seems like a cord unwinding
   From a turn-stile fast to the ground,
And each year new scenes we are finding,
   As we keep on walking around;
We get farther out in the shadows,
   With our life-chord trailed on the ground,
Till at length we have crossed life's meadows,
   And the strange chord is all unwound.

WHAT THE SPIRITS TOLD ME.

NOTE.—This poem was written in the old home in Hardscrabble, ten years ago, and while I was living a bachelor life among the dear old hills where first I saw the greedy world. I have followed the spirit's advice.

Last night sitting weak and weary,
   In my home, so lone and dreary—
Where the voice of gentle woman never falls upon my ear.
   By the dim light on the table, I was writing a strange fable,
Hoping thereby to be able to make life less cold and drear.
Ah, the world knows not the struggles, nor the sad discouraged tear
     Dropping on the hopes I bury
     Every day throughout the year.

All my loved ones death has taken,
And my heart by grief is shaken,
And the old house seems as lonely, sad and gloomy as the
tomb;
And, while I am sitting napping, all around I hear
strange tapping,
And some unseen power rapping all around the dismal room;
And outside I hear strange noises,
Mingling with the midnight gloom.

"Gentle spirit, if you know me,
Rap in answer, please, and show me
What to write to please the public; for, in truth, I do not
know.
Shall I write of wealth and treasure, worldly sports and
earthly pleasure,
Men of money without measure, dressed in diamonds for
vain show?"
This I asked, and all the spirits
With loud rapping answered, "No!"

"Shall I write of war and plunder,
Battles fierce and cannon's thunder,
Where the nations meet in battle, and the blood of soldiers
flow?
Where rulers fight to gain possession, or seek revenge
for some transgression,
Or to crush men for secession, laying forms of traitors low?"
This I asked those midnight spirits
And again they answered, "No!"

"Shall I write of the oppression
By the men who hold possession
Of this world, which God has given, leaving many in
distress?
Shall I ridicule the powers—tyrants in this world of ours,
Raining wealth on some in showers, while the poor they
sore oppress?"
Scarcely had these words been uttered
When the spirits answered, "yes!"

"Shall I defend the babes of cities,
Born in slums, where no heart pities?
All the world seems closed against them, and their hopes
are dark as night.
Christian men, 'tis true, deplore them, but argue, there
is no room for them,
Shall I write, tyrants, restore them to the place they own
by right?"
And the spirits quickly answered,
"Of these wrongs we bid you write!"

Now the morning winds were blowing,
And the barn-yard cocks were crowing,
When the spirits ceased their rapping, vanished with the
shade of night.
Soon the sun o'er the hills came peeping, and into my
room came creeping,
Shone on me as I sat sleeping, 'woke me with its brilliant
light;
Remembering all the spirits told me:
"Of these wrongs we bid you write!"

WHO LIES HERE.

"Here lies"—the cold tombstone said,
In the garden of the dead,
Underneath the angel's head,
  Carved neatly on the stone—
"Here lies honored William Jones;
Peace to his ashes and bones;
Christ for his sins now atones—
  To heaven he has gone."

Says I to myself—says I,
While reading and passing by,
"How easy it is to lie;
  But who is lying here?
If the tombstone man knew Jones
When carving these marble stones
To mark the place where his bones
  Lie, he lied himself, I fear."

I seldom speak ill of the dead,
But Jones is the man who said
The laborers can be fed
  On one dollar a week;
But it cost him *ten* to dine,
And pay for his costly wine;
But then he could pray, and shine
  In the church—he had cheek.

The stone carving man, I know,
Has quite a mission below,
In telling where people go,
    Who leave in a doubtful state.
Why don't his conscience rebel?
And, sometimes, just up and tell
That some people go to—well,
    It's called sheol of late.

When I am dead and buried,
And to the grave-yard hurried,
I don't want strangers flurried
    By reading this to fag 'em:
"Faraway Moses lies here;"
Because they'll believe it, I fear,
And say to themselves, "Oh, dear,
    Satan will surely gag him!"

GRANDPA'S BABY.

Good land of goshen, our Jennie's got a kid!
Named him after his granddad, so she did,
Like a dutiful daughter; Jennie is that,
Gentle, like her mother, and big and fat,
With her great round eyes that move so slow and true;
I tell you, Jane's equals are very few.
But, good lands, just to think how fast time flies;

Baby, childhood, whiskers—then the man dies.
It seems but yesterday since I went to school,
To parse grammar accordin' to the rule,
And now I'm a granddaddy—good lands of joy!
To think our Jane has a baby boy!
Why, it seems but a week past over my head
Since my sweetheart, Betsey, and I were wed,
And now she's a grandma! and I'm a granddad!
And I'm as lean as the last run of shad,
And my knees wobble when I go out to walk,
And these old snags of teeth bother my talk;
And already the neighbors call me old man,
Tho' I try to be as brisk as I can.
And, good lands of goshen, it seems that I have
One foot in childhood, and one in the grave;
And the rest of life has slip'd through my legs,
Like swift water running between two pegs.
And life seems to be gettin' so awful cold
Since Betsey and I are growing so old;
But I'll sing to our grand-child, nevertheless,
And forget all life's worry and distress:
Hip-per-ty Hop-per-ty, up and down we go!
Toots-el-ly woots-el-ly here we stop—whoa!
Old ginger snap on horseback, here we trot so!
Baby's glad, grandpa's sad—no one will know.

WE ARE BLIND.

No one knows the secret sighing,
  Sobbing, in a neighbor's heart;
No one knows the fond hopes dying,
  No one knows the cruel smart.

No one knows the hungry yearning
  Of a neighbor's cheerless soul;
No one knows how grief is burning
  In the heart where hope grows cold.

None but God knows each desire;
  He knows all things in our mind:
Sees hope fanned by passion's fire,
  Knows that love and hope are blind.

When from loved ones we do sever,
  And to far-off countries go,
If we knew we'd see them never—
  Oh, 'tis better not to know!

If we knew the day and minute
  Death would strike the fatal blow,
Life would have less pleasure in it,
  And 'tis better not to know.

Thus, in darkness, hope is ever
  Building castles in our mind,
Cheering soul with visions clever,
  For, like love, our hope is blind.

In our youth what bright creations
　　Hope will picture in our mind,
Lift us to some lofty station—
　　But alas! our hope is blind.

Hope grows dim as we grow older,
　　Castles crumble in our mind;
Youthful loves grow colder, colder!
　　God have mercy—we are blind!

JILTED.

All I ever loved I lost,
　　All I lost who once loved me;
Life is hardly worth the cost;
　　Why not set this poor soul free?

Friends I had, but thus I proved them:
　　They were friendly until I
Proved by actions that I loved them,
　　When all friendships seemed to die.

The choicest flowers of creation
　　Seem to flourish until I
Give to them my admiration,
　　Then they wither up and die.

So with flowers, so with friends—
　　Other hearts with joy they fill;
Where I love all friendship ends,
　　My affections seem to kill.

LOVE'S YOUNG DREAM.

There's the oddest sort of feelin' a bedoozlin' at one's
    heart,
When the pray'r meetin' is over, an' the girls begin to
    start
Towards the church door, a fussin' an' a fixin' on their
    hats ;
An' your heart begins to flutter in sich orful pittipats.

'Cause there's the girl you're lovin' jist as hard as you
    kin love,
Edgin' up towards your rival, an' you haven't gall to
    move,
An' crowd yourself in between 'em an' jist offer her your
    arm,
'Cause you're not so deuced certain of the love of the
    school marm.

An' so, there you stand a waitin' jist outside the church
    front door,
With your heart a pitti-pattin' 'till your ribs are feelin'
    sore,
An' when the school marm comes at last, an' you're most
    half dead with fright,
Your rival scoops her up an' goes off triumphant in the
    night.

Oh, that orful jealous feelin' that keeps gnawin' at your
soul !
As you walk along behint 'em with your blood a runnin'
cold ;
How you hate that stuck-up rival, an' wish you was big
an' stout
Anuff to throw him down an' pound him, and gouge his
both eyes out.

Oh, I know just what I'm sayin', 'cause I've been there
once myself,
An' I know that orful feelin' when you git laid on the
shelf;
When your heart feels so bedoozled that you hardly sleep
or eat,
An' you don't know if your brains are in your gizzard or
your feet.

An' you go around a mopin' with your eyes a lookin' down,
An' the o'ny thought that's in your head is Mary Ida
Brown;
An' in the spring-time, when the birds all come back again
to nest,
Your mother buys a liver pad for to strengthen up your
chest.

RETROSPECT.

Somehow I never had a wish to be a boy again,
To suffer with stone bruises and little stomach pain;
But if I could go back again and live my childhood o'er,
I'd want to be a little cuss just like I was before;
To be the same old boy I was some thirty years ago,
The little harum scarum the neighbors used to know;
To hunt for squirrels on Sunday, and fish for horned chubs,
To climb the trees for chestnut burs, like little hungry cubs;
But of all the boyish joys and delightful happy moods,
There's none like stealing roasting ears and cook them in
      the woods.

I never shall forget the gang who joined me in the feast,
Who went along to steal the corn, and never cared the least
About the sin committed in the middle of the night,
For we thought that boys could never do anything that's
      right
And good and pious, like Sunday school girls would do,
So we went in for a good time, roast corn and chicken stew;
And some would steal the pots and salt from off the kitchen
      shelf,
And others to the cornfield hie, and each one help himself
To neighbor Crawford's early corn, that dear, delicious food,
Then roast the ears like cannibals, on top of burning wood.

Then after the feast was over, and cobs were gnawed off
      clean,
Would begin the story telling while lolling on the green;

And while one boy was spinning a legend or home-made
  lie,
We'd lay on our backs so dreamy and look towards the sky.
When Eli Johnson's turn came he'd tell such an awful tale,
We'd all snug up together and lie in a bunch and quail;
He'd tell of the ghosts his father saw 'way beyond the sea,
And headless spooks his mother saw over in Germany;
And there we'd lay and tremble with a tingling in our
  blood,
When we used to steal the roasting ears and cook them in
  the wood.

Where, oh, where, are these boys to-day? Scattered from
  sea to sea;
And some are mouldering in the grave, from every pain set
  free.
Eli is down in Florida with flowers every day;
Jeff. Farley at Pomona in California;
Will Langdon, and little Sammy, and grumbling old Sie
  Fink,
Frank Haslett, Buck Bryan and Skip—all scattered, just
  to think!
And I am scattered some, too, from the scenes of childhood's
  day,
And the faces of that dear old crowd seem so far away;
But, with closed eyes, I see the spot where Eli Johnson
  stood,
The nights we stole the roasting ears and cooked them in
  the wood.

GOING TO MILL.

Man is like an old tow sack,
  Full of little seeds;
Each variety represents
  His good or wicked deeds.

Time is like a reaper,
  Mowing down life's leaves;
Memory is the gleaner,
  Gathering up the sheaves.

All the sheaves are garnered
  Within the busy brain;
When old age comes to thresh them,
  Memory brings them forth again.

Threshed and winnowed out by pain,
  In nature's mill they fall;
Death will pulverize each grain,
  Then claim the sack and all.

Then let us all be neighborly,
  Climbing life's rough hill;
The rich will ride, the poor must walk,
  But all are going to mill.